Tough Girls
Don't Knit

Also by Freda Garmaise

Love Bites

Tough Girls Don't Knit

and other tales of stylish subversion

Freda Garmaise

Little, Brown and Company

Boston   Toronto   London

FIRST EDITION

Book illustration by Milton Glaser

Some of the pieces in this book originally appeared, in somewhat
different form, in the *Village Voice, Ms.,* and *Cosmopolitan* (London).

Lines from "Time does not bring relief" by Edna St. Vincent Millay
are reprinted by permission from *Collected Sonnets,* revised and
expanded edition, Harper & Row, 1988. Copyright 1917, 1945
by Edna St. Vincent Millay.

LIBRARY OF CONGRESS CATALOGING-IN-PUBLICATION DATA

Garmaise, Freda.
Tough girls don't knit and other tales of stylish subversion /
Freda Garmaise. — 1st ed.
p. cm.
ISBN 0-316-30440-9
I. Title.
PN6162.G35 1990
814'.54 — dc20   89-13549
                                                      CIP

10 9 8 7 6 5 4 3 2 1

FG

Designed by Barbara Werden

*Published simultaneously in Canada
by Little, Brown & Company (Canada) Limited*

PRINTED IN THE UNITED STATES OF AMERICA

For my daughters,
Tina, Bex, and Sophie

*Addresses are given to us to
conceal our whereabouts.*

— Saki

Contents

Contents

Tough Girls
Don't Knit

Personal Belongings —
An Introduction

"Isn't that your ex-wife?" the man inquired of my voice.

"No," my ex-husband said, turning the radio off. "It isn't."

When my daughters, visiting their father at the time, reported this incident, I reminded them that once their father would have been proud to claim me as his own.

The skepticism that greeted this remark annoyed me. But, to be fair, it was understandable — the girls are so used to their father disassociating himself from me (even when we were together) that it was difficult for them to imagine a time when he might have done otherwise.

On the other hand, I frequently refer to him on the air and in print in my lighthearted attempts to add to the fund of human knowledge — something he chooses to characterize as an attempt to get cheap laughs.

Just the same, you might expect my daughters to reproach him for denying me like that, but such disclaimers run in the family.

The children reminded me, for example, of the time when my youngest daughter, giggling helplessly on the first night of the school play, managed to infect with uncontrollable laughter all the other members of the cast, as well as the help backstage. The production, months in the mounting, was reduced to shambles, causing the mother of the star to ask me: "That was your child, wasn't it, spoiling it for my daughter and everyone else?"

I chose to murmur something indistinct in reply, but there was no doubt my mumbles carried a note of dissent.

I, in turn, can point to the time when I had a slight collision with another car and the crook driving it was seized with a maniacal determination to prove the damage was worse than it was.

Naturally, I took him to task for the absurdity of his claims, pointing out that only someone with the mental equipment of an insane criminal would make them in the first place.

His children and mine witnessed the entire affair.

"Is that your mother?" his asked.

"Not really," mine replied.

Of course, when the chips are down, we all stick together. But it is sometimes difficult to reach agreement about when the chips *are* down. And even if such agreement is reached, betrayal is still possible with the excuse that any hint of a bond might make matters more explosive.

Perhaps you have never turned your back on your relatives; but like most of us, you have probably not been above rejecting an object on the grounds that, despite years of faithful service, it lacked the distinction to be associated with your person. Recall, for example, that overwhelming feeling of having to sever all connection when the headwaiter asked of the cheap but reliable article: "Your umbrella, madam?"

Sometimes we are right not to acknowledge certain articles. I remember hanging back when my geography teacher held up a contour map and asked the maker to come forward: "The owner of this has obviously used it to sop up sausage grease, and, given the level of the work, I must say it's as good a use as any for it."

Rightly or wrongly, we are living in a world where your personal belongings can, as my mother would have put it, "show you up" if not ruin your life.

I still think of a painful incident that took place when I was flying home from Morocco and I struck up one of those madly cosmopolitan chats ("They say the cocaine in the Ukraine is something else again . . .") with a suave French architect.

As we were about to land, I experienced a fit of loathing for my luggage.

We were down to the last pieces on the carousel and as my navy nylon set passed for the third time, he asked: "Zees must be yours, non?"

"Non," I said, preparing to pretend mine was lost by the airline rather than have it compared to his handsome canvas-and-leather *bagages*. Then I remembered mine was stuffed with all those bargains from *le souk* in Marrakech: "I mean, oui! Stupide moi! C'est le hotel maid's. Mine was lost, so I borrowed hers . . ."

He gave me a look that mingled doubt with distaste and I could see that the image he had of me, as a jet-hopping sophisticate, had evaporated. No further mention was made of the taxi we were to have shared (or the life that would have followed it), and we went our separate ways.

5

Perhaps I should have run after him, crying: "C'est mes valises, n'est-ce pas? Pourquoi permettez ces lousy choses to come entre nous?"

But I didn't. I went home, unpacked, and threw my matched set out.

But, as you see, it lived on.

Well, that's what happens when you get paid to tell the world about the stuff you never had the nerve to call your own. It attaches itself to you. After a while you even feel a certain pride of ownership.

That may not be the case with you. In going through my personal belongings, you may find something of yours. If you do and you don't want to own up to it, it's okay.

I already did it for you.

Shoppers of the World Unite!

To take the measure of a person, I have often asked: Do you dance? Do you vote? Do you like Graham Greene? But in the future I intend to ask: "Do you shop?"

I imagine myself at a party directing this inquiry to someone (an economist, critic, editor) whose epic sweep of mind can be seen in his contemptible ties and shoes. He will answer that no, he does not, and offer the fact that he hates to shop as yet another credential of his superiority. Asshole, I will say, if I am feeling bold; how can you deliberately deprive yourself of means to exercise your ability to select, bargain, experience the new, relive the old, and give your life the rich detail that the thoughtless cut of your suit and hair shows you are severely lacking? Get out there and shop, I will say to him, and then come back and talk to me about price structures or the future of publishing.

We all shop (even he does). But less than fifteen percent (my figure) of the earth's inhabitants do it well. And doing it well is to be *mindful* of it; to be aware at all times that as a daily activity it is uniquely constituted to make us aware of ourselves and the world around us.

But because we do it automatically, resentfully, indifferently, impatiently, excessively, nervously, hysterically, and, above all, thoughtlessly, we deprive ourselves of shopping's real benefits. Our willful indifference has far-reaching results, bringing us trade deficits and wars as well as cheeseboards and sheets we detest. Yet great shopping ("Where did you get this unbelievable egg timer?") is only acknowledged in private circles.

"Neither Bush nor Dukakis recognizes shoppers," I complained to a shopper.

"Shabbas? Dukakis recognizes Shabbas. Kitty makes him."

When I told her I'd said "shoppers," she said: "Oh, you mean consumers." Well, no I don't. Consumers are interested in getting value for their money and may not even *like* shopping since, for them, it may be a tedious quest in search of quality, fair play, and honesty. Shoppers may care about those things, too, but not necessarily. They may tolerate inferior quality for some other attribute (cuteness, for example), they may indulge in foul play and cheat in pursuit of the prize on the bargain table, but to them shopping is a path of discovery, the route to enlightenment — whether it leads them to the magic lamp in a dusty corner of the shop or not. Shoppers shop for its own sake — as a means to be out and about, to check up on the world, to renew themselves — not just to find something to buy.

But if the word *shopper* has a bad name, it is because those to whom it is usually applied are considered greedy and ridiculous. The Nancy Reagans and the Imelda Marcoses have discredited the term, but they are not shoppers.

They are spenders. They do not browse, poke around, snoop, pounce, discover. They order. They acquire. They could just as well shop from a catalog or TV screen. Unlike true shoppers, they must have money. True shoppers like to have money too (no denying that), but they can shop without it.

I fell in with a bunch of true shoppers in California. Living by the skin of their teeth, they buy everything at the thrifts — furniture, household articles, books, clothing, major appliances. Being with them was like being in several different decades at once and simultaneously experiencing the Depression dinette set, the couch from the forties, and the edition of *The Great Gatsby* issued while F. Scott Fitzgerald was still alive. Particularly thrilling to me, in these cholesterol-conscious times, was the opportunity I had to extract lettuce and fish from the big, fat fifties fridge built to house dry martinis and three-inch steaks.

Of course you can be an enterprising, imaginative, indefatigable, even prophetic shopper and never go near the thrifts; but unlike the fan in the Deanna Durbin frock and ankle socks, who puts into perspective the sea of jeans at the rock concert, you will never be able to offer those around you that remembrance of things past that brings the present into focus. And that's what makes the thrift shopper the greatest on earth.

I am not a good shopper. I am too timid, too unsure, too lazy. I am touched by the packages of panty hose fanned out to lure me into the neighborhood lingerie store, but I am afraid to go in for fear of being bullied into buying something. If I were a great shopper, I would risk getting stuck with a pair of cocoa knee-highs to preserve that greatest of all shopping traditions — contact between buyer and seller. Similarly, when I am in the mall and feeling guilty because

I should be doing more than buying a packet of pins (in order to justify all the fountains and flowers and marble resting places), I shall remember that even the purchase of pins is unwarranted in this place, with its pseudomarket air that defiles everything the ancient practice of shopping is about.

For years I thought I *was* a great shopper because I had great clothes. But that was when I was a fashion editor and my wardrobe consisted of the liveliest of the manufacturers' samples rejected by middle-of-the-road store buyers as too original, too avant-garde for general consumption. I congratulated myself on my taste and smart buying habits, forgetting that what buyers refuse is usually the best the manufacturer has to offer. When I had to buy my clothes in stores like everyone else, my wardrobe quickly became a reflection of the numbing selection made on my behalf. I became a dull and listless shopper. Or perhaps it would be truer to say I was revealed as the dull and listless shopper I always was. Up until then, my wardrobe distracted from my substandard level of shopping. Now, it joined my other purchases, confirming the insulting opinion most stores have of me — that I am not interested in the new, the beautiful, the original, or even the sensible.

Thanks to the substandard performance I and millions like me give, stores keep getting more and more boring. Perhaps Bloomingdale's *would* be like no other store in the world if its buyers were encouraged by lively, aware shoppers who continually challenge them to be different by refusing merchandise that could be found elsewhere. As it is, Bloomingdale's is indistinguishable from other stores, despite those spectaculars when the store is transformed for China month. To the true shopper, these extravaganzas seem no more than an elaborate ruse to sell the dragon-stenciled tote bag.

In an effort to improve, I have decided to shop even when I do not need anything, even when I am broke. (Note: I do not say *buy;* the practice of buying things one cannot afford is a degradation of shopping. No, I talk of scouting the shops, studying the trends, quizzing the clerks — in short, observing the rituals.) I will also ignore the rule that certain things may be inspected only by those who can afford them and I shall insist on examining the Rei Kawakubos. And finally, I will try not to hasten the death of the hunt by buying bargains only in discount stores.

And then perhaps one day I will reach the point where I can look at the teakettle or bathrobe I own without my spirits sagging because it is proof not only of the way I shop, but the way I do most things.

How often have I believed that something outside my life (a bout of Buddhism, regular exercise) could change it, when all the time shopping — already an integral part of existence — was the answer!

Now do you see why I did not account it progress when I read of a man who did shopping for his wife? He wouldn't think of jogging for his wife, would he? No, everyone must shop for herself. For himself. Buying and selling are basic; none of us can afford not to be part of the process. The world is undoubtedly in the shape that it is because men believed themselves above shopping, relied on surrogates to do it, and used the time instead to get into mischief. (Hitler, I am convinced, never shopped. And if there is hope for the Eastern bloc, it is in the fact that, I believe, Gorbachev does.)

Throughout the entire 1988 presidential campaign, no

one saw fit to ask the candidates, "Do you shop?" — although the subject was broached with their wives.

So, Bush went into the White House with nothing known of this vital aspect of his character. There is still time to remedy the situation. Let's get the measure of the president by asking whether *he* actually went out and bought Barbara's birthday present.

For all we know, he could lead us into a future where, having succumbed to labels, we move as automatons from one corporate outlet to another in a grotesque parody of shopping. And as the kinder, gentler nation becomes a duller, meaner, more standardized place, we will remember dimly, perhaps, a happier time — a time full of color and variety, before we betrayed our destiny and the singular fact that we were born to shop.

I Go at a Maddening Pace

The fact that exercise books usually have little literary value doesn't surprise me.

I would expect the authors of such books to be like my old gym teacher Miss Cream, who (despite her belief that books interfered with a girl's development) might have written one to put across her view that enlightenment awaited those who mastered the wall bars. She called me "The Slacker" because I preferred reading to knee bends, and used me as a handy example of how not to vault a horse. My dismal act would be followed by Monica, star of the gym, whose dazzling display of vaulting, jumping, and swinging was offered by Miss Cream as evidence of the heights to which humankind might aspire.

Although I cultivated a slouch and sneered at Monica and her like, I secretly dreamed of inspiring awe in Miss Cream by reading aloud from the classics as I swung from the ropes and turned somersaults. I see now that such displays have only a low freak value; but I have proved, years later, that if it is not possible to get in shape and have a good read, your inspiration to keep fit can still be literary. After decades of failing to find satisfaction with the Jack LaLannes and Jane Fondas, I found my exercise guru in the late, great Russian writer Ivan Turgenev.

Turgenev and I go back to the time when I adapted *Fathers and Sons* for CBC Radio. I cannot tell you how intimate a situation like that can become. By the time I had finished the six episodes, I believed I had written the novel myself — a conviction not shared by my producer, who refused to allow *"Fathers and Sons* by Freda Garmaise, from a story by Ivan Turgenev" to be announced in the credits.

Once I had cashed the check for the adaptation, I might have thought Turgenev could do nothing more for me had I not read his biography and been struck by the fact that, in little ways, at any rate, we were so alike: when he was caught in an uprising in Paris, it was the selling of cigars and cocoa to the protesters that stayed in his mind (I am apt to dwell on the minor detail at the expense of the large event), and when he wanted a reminder of his beloved, he begged for her fingernail clippings (I, too, have thought of these snippets as a suitable keepsake). You may feel these are flimsy resemblances, but they were enough to convince me — when I read how Turgenev walked up and down his cell four hundred times a day for exercise after the czar imprisoned him — that pacing would be good for me, too.

Since Turgenev was a rich landowner — his estate covered twenty villages and boasted five thousand muzhiks — his imprisonment fitted his station in life: all the champagne he could drink, visits from friends, rich foods, and so on. We can assume that he was not pacing (as other prisoners might) out of terror, boredom, or rage, but to work off the results of excessive living, work up a few ideas on life and writing, and perhaps learn Polish — which, apart from the last item, would be my aims exactly.

On that first morning, I felt a bit of a fool walking up and down my apartment; but then resolution took hold as I began to feel that nothing I had ever done — not aerobics, calisthenics, jazz ballet, or yoga — had ever so suited my restless nature and wandering mind as pacing. Perhaps Turgenev had someone to do it for him, but I couldn't count and pace, so I timed myself instead. Never in the annals of my personal exercising have I wished to prolong the workout — but within a week (covering the hall and partway across the living room, about thirty feet), I went from ten minutes to one hour!

My style varies: sometimes I saunter, sometimes I stroll, sometimes I drag my feet, sometimes I wiggle my hips athletically, sometimes I stride, sometimes I sashay like Mae West, sometimes I pump my shoulders like John Wayne, and sometimes I walk so fast that the furniture flashes past me in a blur.

Since taking up pacing, I have lost weight (a pound or two), put a spring in my step, brought a flush to my cheeks, added a sparkle to my eye, and convinced myself that I've taken the right steps at last to produce a significant work. Tolstoy, who was not known to pace, thought Turgenev was a better writer than he. Too bad Virginia Woolf's dead, or I might have wrung a similar confession about me from her.

When I think of the centuries and centuries that pacing has been thought of as a bad habit — like biting your nails or grinding your teeth — and deliberately repressed as neurotic, compulsive, unproductive behavior, I could weep. Who is to know how many brilliant schemes have been lost

15

forever because someone said, "For God's sake, sit down —
acting like a caged lion isn't going to get you anywhere."

Sitting around waiting for lightning to strike, I would
have thought, is more suited to the Eastern mind than ours.
Believe me, I know what I am talking about. I have em-
barked on those programs that have you begin by emptying
your mind. I have no trouble doing that; but once the super-
ficial stuff moves out, nothing of any substance moves in.

The same thing may happen even with those Westerners
who are deeply Eastern, like the poet Allen Ginsberg, who I
once saw doing tai chi on PBS and sharing (through a voice-
over) what went through his mind — commonplace stuff, as
I recall, like worry about nuclear annihilation and the rent
and whether or not the kettle was turned off. You can be sure
I'll be withholding insights gained through pacing until I am
sure they're worth spreading around.

Perhaps Allen should take up pacing. He might find it
offers more of a mental workout than tai chi does, since you
don't have to think about the moves you're making — possibly the greatest advantage pacing has as an exercise.

Mind you, it is just as well to pay attention to certain
details of pacing, like dressing for it. I was never aware of
what I wore to pace until my daughter stopped by and I answered the door, as she described it, "wearing nothing but
sneakers and an officious air" — a reference to the clipboard
I was carrying to make a note should inspiration strike. Now
I make sure I've at least put on a T-shirt — and socks too,
after I developed a blister on my heel from pacing a mara-
thon.

No other special facilities are required. Lack of space isn't
an obstacle. Even if you take only a couple of steps before

retracing them, or have to weave in and out of the furniture, you can do it. Don't forget, pacing thrives on confinement.

Those close to me seem to have mixed feelings about my pacing. I overheard my daughter remark to a friend, "As long as it makes her happy"; but I suspect the friend thinks pacing is a waste of time, because she suggested that I tie dusters to my feet so I could polish the floor while doing it. The thought of degrading pacing by using it to houseclean is bad enough; never mind that it would bring me down to the level of one of Turgenev's serfs, when I look upon myself as part of his class. And while it is true that I am not a Russian aristocrat or rich landowner, if Ivan were around today, he wouldn't be, either.

While my daughters indulge my need to pace, they feel I don't go far enough for real benefit and that I should carry weights while doing it. "Books will do," they say.

So far I have not followed this suggestion, although an editor I know attempts to overcome the damage of those hours spent sitting at his desk by rising with armfuls of the *Encyclopaedia Britannica* every time he leaves it. The sight of this man staggering about under loads of books has, apparently, raised serious questions as to his fitness for publishing, and he is said to be risking dismissal.

I feel lucky to be a home worker when I see how difficult it is to fit one's own exercise remedies into the corporate world, and that even in the small, independent firm there are problems. Recently, in conversation with a travel agent, I noticed she was continually making faces (hideous grimaces, belligerent pouts, and raised eyebrows), and every so often sharply drawing in her breath. None of this, I discovered, had anything to do with my inquiry about what to expect in Helsinki in June, but was a combination of facial isometrics (to obviate future face-lifts) and abdominal exercises (to flatten the stomach), a regimen she confessed she may have to drop because of its disconcerting effect on the customer.

If you are powerful enough, it doesn't matter what people think. A Wall Street man who heard symphony conductors live long lives through raised-arm exercising now spends part of each day conducting recordings his secretary selects for the frenzy of their scores. The man is not a music lover ("Even less of one now," he grimly remarks, finally lowering his arms after doing the Fifth), and if he lives as long as Toscanini, you can be sure Beethoven won't get the credit for it.

I am only too happy to give thanks to Turgenev for the transformation in my life and to urge others to follow my course. Not that many will. To convince the public, I'd have to show a dynamic, Jamie Lee Curtis–like result, and to look at me, you'd never know how great pacing is . . . mere measurements don't tell the story.

Okay, so you wouldn't put Turgenev in the same league as Jake (Jamie Lee's personal trainer), whose full title — Body by Jake — implies a godlike propensity. But can he keep Jamie at it? Will she grow weary, will the flesh turn to flab, the muscles to string?

The recidivist rate for exercising (those who take it up and drop it) is extremely high. But with pacing, I have found that far from growing tired of it, I cannot do it enough. Sometimes the urge is so strong I just have to excuse myself from the dinner party and go to the bathroom and pace. At such moments I think of Turgenev pacing in his cell and then breaking off for caviar and champagne, and I go back to the table renewed.

"Who's ready for seconds?" the hostess is asking.

"I am," I say. Why not? Turgenev has given me a lifetime to work it off.

We Have Ways to Make You Watch

I am standing naked in front of Robert MacNeil, probably as good a way as any to protest the unrelenting fairness of *The MacNeil/Lehrer NewsHour*. In any event, if one day Mac-Neil, having politely extracted opinions from right and left, looks directly into the camera and shouts, "For God's sake, put some clothes on!" you will know why. But even if he skips this stage, I trust you will remember that it was I who provoked him when he finally snaps at Elliott Abrams, "You are a sickening human being and your opinions disgust me."

You may think it madness to believe that *how* you watch television as much as what you watch can influence its outcome. But you would be totally convinced if you could have seen the consternation I caused when, desperate to be the center of attention, I announced at a dinner party of TV people, "TV should always be watched standing." There was a shocked reaction. Voices were raised. Someone said such a viewing posture could lead to TV being treated as casually, as *disrespectfully*, as radio, because once people were on their feet, what was to stop them from going about their business and treating TV as just something on in the background? That, everyone agreed, would be the deepest possible abuse of the medium.

What they meant, of course, was the deepest possible abuse of *them*. What greater blow to the producers of TV could there be than to have viewers acting as if *nothing* on it could possibly merit more than a casual glance, let alone sitting down?

Knowing this, you'd think people wouldn't mind staying on their feet. But to many, the thrill of getting on with their lives as Cagney and Lacey vainly try to attract their attention soon wears thin.

Some people believe that it is only by *sitting down* in front of the TV that you can hope to accomplish anything — learning Greek to the accompaniment of *M*A*S*H* reruns, getting through Tolstoy's *War and Peace* with the help of *L.A. Law*.

Despite TV's proved usefulness, you may ask at this point: why turn the set on at all? And the answer to that is: if you don't, you could become like those people who won't have a set in the house at all and spend mealtimes discussing quantum physics with their children in Flemish. These children grow up so hungry for TV and so convinced they can improve the rest of us with it that they become producers, perpetuating such mind-numbing shows as those on the life of the fern.

So for the sake of succeeding generations (if nothing else), it's important to be a TV watcher — always remembering, of course, how essential it is to exert control.

One way to do it is in the way you dress. Now, when TV first came in, we knew we were watching it by what we

21

were wearing. We would get out of our sheath dresses, girdles, and high-heeled shoes and change into our capri pants, blouses, and high-heeled mules. But since those days, we have blunted that awareness by wearing the same clothes for TV as we do for everything else. As I have already shown, it wasn't until I took off my habitual working garment, a grubby bathrobe, that I saw a way of changing *MacNeil/Lehrer.* You may well wish to do something more elaborate; but may I suggest that until you work out a wardrobe-to-watch-in, you at least watch with a hat on, or something tight.

Watching TV informally, as most of us do, only makes it more mindless. If the more you watch, the more pointless your life seems, then turning the activity into an event (as it was in the early days, when sets were scarce and parties were held around them) could be the answer. *Great Performances* would lend itself to a musical soiree, with evening dress required of guests, who would be seated on small gold chairs to watch Solti conduct the Philharmonic. If you habitually talk back to the TV and are obviously keen on having input, then get the gang over for an après-Oprah party — when she's off the air, you take over.

My favorite way of watching at the moment is to do it while on the phone. Tellyphoning can be done in a number of different ways: both parties watching the same program, both watching different programs, or by jumping around the dial — starting from opposite ends and meeting in the middle is fun.

Tellyphoning is a practice I copied from my daughters. But ever since the time I lured them to an educational show by pretending it carried the warning "The following program shows actual mating practices — parental discretion is advised" and then they waited an hour to catch the copulation

22

on a show about rock formation, they have never allowed me to influence their viewing habits.

In those days, I still believed there was something to be learned from the programs on TV — but then *I* was on it, on a local talk show. Once, when a friend of my daughter's visited, I was anxious not to ruin my public image with my disreputable dishabille (that bathrobe again), so I flitted, phantomlike, from the room when the kids entered it, causing the visiting child to declare: "Your mother seems more *real* on TV." That remark gave rise to the fear that besets certain tribes who believe the camera steals away your soul — could I be a mere shadow while my real life languished in some electronic time warp? And could I get it back one day with the appropriate viewing posture and outfit? Who knows? But it is certainly another good reason to watch how I watch. So . . .

I am sitting in sequins in front of Jane Pauley, scrutinizing her through binoculars.

C'est le Style Farceur

"Surely, you're not going out in that?" my mother would exclaim as I primped for the party in the beaded cerise dance frock she'd abandoned fifteen years before. But of course I was, hoping that my ensemble would provoke the more flattering remark, "Only *you* could get away with it." More often than not, I was likely to overhear someone say, "*What is she wearing now?*" But this was the time when the world was still measuring chic by the twinset and pearls.

In my own modest way, I anticipated the swinging sixties. Determined to be different, I depended on the thrift shop for the bowler or the boa, customized the off-the-rack item (Mother's reaction: "It's a crime the way you spoiled that new two-piece"), and eventually even took to sewing from scratch. My aim was not to turn the fashion world on its ear. All I hoped was that the cerise beads (or whatever else I had on my back) would identify me as a unique and original person. The sort of person, in fact, who would be welcome in Paloma Picasso's circle. Even today, and even if I had the money, I can tell you I wouldn't fall back on the *tailleur* of Yves Saint Laurent or the steamy seaming of Azzedine Alaia to do it.

I have yet to meet Paloma, but as a radio interviewer I have encountered many celebrities. And my clothes have been perfect for the job. If I'd been on TV, I might have been pressured, for the sake of credibility, into something more conventional. But listeners can't see you, so I was free to strive for effect when I was on display during my celebrity encounters.

One of my first interviews was with Pierre Cardin. I was wearing a raincoat said to have belonged to a Finnish flapper and aviatrix. It was a capacious garment that ballooned about me. "Does eet convairt to a parachute?" Cardin inquired. "*Non*," I replied, "not even to a *parapluie*." You'd think that such a snappy retort would have rated me an invitation to Maxim's. But it did not. Tom Conti was moved to ask, "Is it warm enough?" as he helped me into the army surplus coat that was supposed to protect against chemical warfare but proved a poor barrier against the November chill. "Yes," I lied, not wishing to be thought a fool for fashion and hoping he'd shift onto something like, "What are you doing for dinner?" But Mr. Conti's concern for my welfare stopped with the coat.

Still, even if my fashion sense hasn't yet put me on a personal footing with the famous, I never felt it let me down until I went to interview Annie Leibovitz, photographer of the stars. I turned up somewhat earlier than expected in my Isak Dinesen cloche, my Great Depression (period, not mood) cardigan, and print dress, and was greeted with, "You must be the new bookkeeper." It was a dreadful moment and I blame Madonna, Boy George, and others who have popularized fashion lawlessness in the common flock, causing all-out anarchists such as myself to be mistaken for persons from the mainstream.

Fortunately, this was an isolated incident. My wardrobe is usually wild enough to have people wondering how I even got into the media. Certainly it was a question that puzzled my ex-husband. We met during my period of deliberate dishevelment. I like to think I anticipated punk chic (I definitely had runs in my stockings), but I took my cue from that line, "A sweet disorder in the dress kindles in clothes a wantonness." In other words, untidiness was next to sexiness. My husband fell madly in love with me in the mistaken belief that I looked the way I did because I spent no time on myself and once I did I'd be a knockout. Even after he found out that my air of slovenly turbulence took hours to assemble, and that once washed, brushed, and ready for bed I was a lot less alluring, he married me anyway. And I married him because although he was an ex-flyer, newspaperman, and Mr. Macho, his mother had taught him how to use a sewing machine. Moreover, he bought me one and taught me.

He saw the machine as the tool to reform my deranged fashion sense, and talked a lot about pure, clean line and form. In pursuit of this, our first attempt was one of those geometric triangular minis so popular in the sixties. It didn't matter that we cut it from a stiff, cheap fabric in a lurid color, because this was only a demo dress to prepare me for making my wedding gown. I wanted to be romantic in old lace and intended to adapt two tablecloths for the purpose. But I'd reckoned without some immovable stains and my sewing skills were unequal to maneuvering around them. I ended up with less usable lace than you'd need for a fair-size hankie. Since everything else in my wardrobe was from the derelict-chic period and there was neither time nor money to get another dress, I ended up getting married in the demo. Ever after that my husband referred to me as "the daring young bride in the lime green trapeze."

That image, as it turned out, may have been the kindest he had of me during our entire marriage. Even though I was an assiduous user of the sewing machine, it was in the service of *my* fashion fantasies, not his. Among other things, he deplored the fact that I always made loose garments (tubes or tents, depending on figure fluctuation) and, because I couldn't wait to get the results on my back, never finished anything properly. Once, we went to lunch with his boss, who, seeing me rush shortsightedly past his table, caught my sleeve in his hand. It stayed there, having been held only by tacking stitches.

Such fashion faux pas were becoming somewhat burdensome to my husband, who'd switched from writing news to churning out publicity and was sinking deeper into the corporate world. My fashion taste, as much as anything else, brought out the basic and irreconcilable differences between us that ultimately led to divorce.

Since then, no one has tried to suppress my fashion whims. I have dressed as I pleased. Something, I realized, I vowed to do from quite a young age. I couldn't have been more than ten when I was paraded past the open coffin containing old Mrs. Groots, a neighbor of ours. I was surprised to see her in her Sunday crepe and diamanté brooch.

"What's she wearing that for?" I asked.

"She's going to meet her maker," Mom replied.

It struck me that she'd be overdressed for the occasion. God and his entourage always seemed to be in dishabille.

Shouldn't Mrs. Groots be in her nightie? Apparently she had decreed otherwise and had carefully specified the crepe for her laying out.

I admired that. I knew Mrs. Groots treasured the figure she cut and would want God to know right off where she stood on style, no matter the prevailing dress code. That must have been when I decided I would not leave my fashion fate up to others. For a few more years, matters were in my mother's hands — until I defied her. I cinched my blazer in with a belt for peplum flare.

"Where do you think you're going, looking like that?" she asked.

"To school," I said. And I did. And a fashion rebel was born.

Me and My Shadow, You and Yours

When a friend told me about how she was carrying on with Tom Berenger, I felt a sickening stab of jealousy. She owns the video of *Someone to Watch over Me*, and has watched it so many times she now feels Tom is watching over *her*, which is a terrible thing to hear when you happen to be in the midst of a relationship with the man yourself.

"He's my little moving pinup, aren't you, honey?" she asked, patting Tom's behind as he walked off to a stakeout. She also fast-forwards to cut out Mimi Rogers, freezes frames so she can kiss Tom, and often replays bits, chuckling, "Do it to me one more time."

It was terrible to see him stripped of his dignity, reduced to a plaything. This was not an isolated incident — women all over America are abusing major stars. I heard of a woman who did appalling things with Arnold Schwarzenegger, and then taunted Maria Shriver with them while she was trying to do her *Sunday Today* show. Even the older generation is behaving disrespectfully. One woman profaned the memory of Cary Grant by appearing before him in a housedress, without her dentures.

I saw *Someone to Watch over Me* only once, but the image I carried away of Tom was enough for me to build a life for the two of us. For months afterward, he lived for me, for my impromptu suppers of sauerkraut and smelts, the way I recited Emily Dickinson, the way I walked, talked, *breathed*. I liked the way he looked in an overcoat, but once I had seen him on that VCR, he wasn't *mine* anymore; he was a puppet manipulated for someone else's convenience. I no longer wanted or needed his love and admiration. Things were over between us. After a short spell alone to get my head sorted out, I let Gene Hackman move in.

Gene is also available on video. I do not have a VCR, but should I ever get one, I don't rule out its use in our relationship (after all, if it had not been for film, we would not have met in the first place) — as long as it enhances the very special, very unusual thing we share together.

I have built one-on-one relationships ever since I took my first lover, the French movie star Jean Gabin, at the age of twelve. He was already middle-aged, but that mattered as little as the fact that we didn't speak the same language. Subtitles flashed in my head as he spoke, and I even began to pick up a little French. Once, unaware that I was not alone, I kissed his picture, passionately declaring, *"Je t'adore"*; my kid brother said, "Shut it yourself." He was always a brutish boy. He had a VCR and is undoubtedly using it to do disgusting things to Debra Winger.

My fantasy life is not only threatened by the outside world but, ironically, by the very way I earn my living. Michael Caine was obsessed with me (he loved my lightning cockney wit — so much faster than his). We might still be together if I hadn't had to interview him for radio, where I was expected to shut up and let him do the talking.

I met him in his hotel. He was smoking a cigar (something he'd never done in our lives together) as he talked of the frustration of growing daffodils in Beverly Hills (you planted them in the morning and they were up by the afternoon), and of his intention to return to England, where bulbs matured as nature intended.

"You're English, aren't you?" he asked me.

"I used to be," I replied enigmatically.

"You ought to try it again," he advised. "Now that Mrs. Thatcher's running things."

I felt a cold chill. Mrs. Thatcher and I have often met in open debate. She has felt the lash of my tongue, the force of my argument. She has withered under my contempt. The queen, who can't stand her either, will probably make me a dame for showing Maggie up for what she is. It was sickening to think that during our most intimate moment, Michael had betrayed me with admiring thoughts of her.

"Good-bye, Mr. Caine," I said coldly, as I took my leave — although I had called him Michael throughout the interview. That, of course, is in accordance with the rules of radio, which require that the broadcaster give the listener the impression that she is on a first-name basis with celebrities. He hadn't called *me* anything. I had thought of impressing my name on him by getting him to say "Freda, Freda, Freda" as a sound check and keeping the tape to play over at certain ecstatic moments. But there would be no more moments now that I knew where he stood with Mrs. T.

Most would call me lucky to be able to encounter my

phantoms in the flesh. But for those of us who have an active fantasy life such meetings can only be disruptive. Even if stars don't disillusion you with their political outlook, they are always shorter and thinner. All except Danny DeVito, whose shortness was larger than life when we met, and who made me feel taller and more willowy than any man ever has. This meeting might have led to a fantasy affair; but I knew it would mean dealing with Danny's wife, Rhea Perlman, whom I'd seen as Carla on *Cheers* and who I knew would make a nuisance of herself.

I tried to caution my daughter Sophie against mixing fantasy and reality the time she successfully begged me to let her come along when I interviewed Matt Dillon. Matt was, after all, her first serious romance. I feared for the consequences of their meeting. At first, I thought the magic was preserved, because when he asked her, "How ya doin'?" she could do no more than nod her head. Later, though, I heard her making fun of him, repeating how I'd asked if there was a story he'd like to see made into a picture and he'd said, "There's a lot of good books out there." His encounter with Sophie could be the basis for a Matt Dillon movie — a mood piece about a phantom made flesh — and the camera could zoom in for a closing shot of his cigarette butt, which she keeps to this day in a mother-of-pearl pillbox.

Although it might turn my stomach, it wouldn't surprise me to see a study coming out of the relics collected by groupies: one has only to think of how Elvis's fans clamored for the scarves he used to wipe off his sweat during performances. Elvis, too, had fans who followed him around. One woman left her husband so she could do so. Now she may be among those who have spotted Elvis at convenience stores; once you become accustomed to real-life sightings of your fantasy man, you're not going to give them up just because he's dead.

I would not have left my husband to be near Harrison Ford (even if I hadn't thought we were close enough already, how could I afford such a high-rent neighborhood?); but I wish now that I had spread the word that he was responsible for the breakup of our marriage — as, in a sense, he was. It was the thought of Harrison working off the stresses of stardom with his carpentry skills, turning out dining-room tables and cocktail cabinets, as much as his style as a lover, that showed up my husband in such a poor light. If I had cited Harrison — he was Han Solo then — as home breaker, at least I could have kept my children begging for details. As it was, interest in my plight quickly waned ("Do we have to talk about you and Dad *again*, Mom?").

I would say nine out of ten women comfort themselves with phantom lovers during marriage. Some even try to marry them in the first place. The Arrow Collar Man was nothing more than a drawing. He only existed on paper. Yet in one month in the 1920s he received seventeen thousand letters (more mail than Rudolph Valentino), many of which included marriage proposals. What replies did those eager applicants pray for — "Darling, I accept your proposal and enclose myself herein"?

This paper doll remained an idol for twenty-six years (1905 to 1931), with his style changing gradually enough for women to adjust. Not like today. I had barely started one of those "older woman/younger man" flings with Kevin Costner, the hothead kid brother I'd fallen for in *Silverado*, when suddenly he popped up as the over-the-hill baseball player in *Bull Durham* and overnight became too old to play a part in my life.

Of course, I understand that my phantom lovers must be free to accept a movie role even if it means destroying my love for them. After all, my rejection of them does not threaten their very existence, as I believe the VCR does. Can it be long before there are video games for women to play that allow them to go further than they ever dreamed and customize their dreamboats ("Hey, get a load of Nick Nolte on Fred Astaire's body!"), thus making heroes into laughingstocks?

To some women, bringing out the night sweats in William Hurt when he thinks of what they can do to him on video is a way to give men their comeuppance; but believe me, we are only shortchanging ourselves. We need the phantom man. Does it make sense for us to thin his ranks further and reduce our selection, which is already naturally pruned by his appearance on the talk show ("I thought you were so independent, James Woods, yet you behaved like a fawning sycophant") or by other objectionable behavior ("Okay, Jeff Bridges, play around with her — just don't expect to find me here when you come back")? Disillusion always waits; we don't have to manufacture it.

The VCR cannot do other than cause us to strip the rich mine of celebrities, and we may have to regress to an old flame (reissuing him in only his most attractive aspects), have squalid encounters with historical figures ("Okay, so you slept around, George, but if Martha can take it, so can I"), or laboriously build a fantasy affair on the clue or two we picked up from the man sitting opposite on the subway train.

A sad state of affairs, and one that can be avoided if we remember to ask not what we can do *to* our phantom lovers but what they can do *for* us. For it is probably only the fantasy man who can make you the dream woman you know yourself to be. When you are protecting his shadow, you are protecting your own.

A Kiss on the Hand

I once had my hand kissed by a count who thought I might write his wife's memoirs. As his immaculate lips brushed my knuckles, I was aware that he was getting a whiff of dishwashing detergent and a close-up of my Timex Easy Reader. Those details probably convinced him that I wasn't the person to deliver authentic accounts of giddy nights with the crowned heads of Europe and fun-filled days on millionaires' yachts; it didn't matter, though, because I wouldn't have taken the job anyway.

I had no interest in telling the countess's life story (at least not one she'd want to read) once she'd spoken of her affection for Franco and voiced her regret that he was so widely misunderstood. Just for fun, I thought I'd let her ramble on, in the belief that she was impressing me, and then I'd deliver my stinging rejection. But before I could, the count was saying he'd be in touch, kissing my hand again, and having me ushered out the front door onto Park Avenue.

It is at times like these that you realize how useful hand

kissing can be and what a shame it is that all the wrong people do it. Of course, that is no longer true in Poland, where the gesture, which has always reeked of privilege, has been taken up by steelworkers and salt miners, signaling solidarity as the raised fist never has.

The Poles are kissing hands to annoy the Russians and Polish hard-liners, and although the Polish aristocracy (or what is left of it) must be pleased to see Communism put in its place, there could be dismay, too, that the gesture is available to whoever cares to use it.

The British upper crust have always considered hand kissing foreign and distasteful. They would be inclined to be cavalier rather than gallant in using kissing for social significance. I suppose my father could be said to have aped them when he sang

> *The working class can kiss my arse,*
> *I've got the foreman's job at last.*

But if he had sung

> *The working class can kiss my hand,*
> *I've got the foreman's job as planned.*

his words would have spoken of advancement by cool calculation (rather than limp seniority) — advancement achieved, moreover, with the help of his staff, whose collaboration could be counted on for further triumphs. In other words, a kiss on the arse will afford momentary exultation but a kiss on the hand could signal a climb to far dizzier heights. Capo di capos in the Mafia demand the hand kiss; and although I wouldn't pretend this alone is responsible for a disciplined and loyal rank and file, or necessary for promotion within it, I have no doubt it plays its part.

Hand kissing, as a courtly gesture, seems to be on the decline in those countries where it once flourished. Recent history suggests the Italians have found bottom pinching more effective. A Frenchman will still kiss a hand, but it is usually his own and involves applying his lips to the tips of his fingers — to signal his appreciation for food or wine. Still, they've done a fair amount of hand kissing in their time. "You've got to start somewhere," Sacha Guitry observed, signifying what sets off Frenchmen from their counterparts in the United States, who, by the time they've kissed a woman's hand, have usually kissed everything else.

That's probably okay with most American women, for whom the thought of hand kissing provokes not so much flutter as fluster: many fear that their hands, groomed or not, don't *deserve* to be kissed, or find that the prospect of lips let loose on them is an unpleasant one.

Not, however, a friend of mine who has had her hand kissed three times in the past month and hopes we are looking at a trend. In fact, she enjoyed the experience so much she now finds herself extending her hand as a matter of course in the hope of it being repeated.

What would she do, I asked, if she didn't want her hand kissed. Kiss his first, she said, claiming it would come as a surprise move and she could do it in a sufficiently dismissive way to discourage him from either returning the salute or contemplating another try in the future.

There are a few hands I'd like to kiss myself. I wish I'd had the chance after I'd interviewed Ricardo Montalban, but as it was, he kissed my hand and murmured, "You are very charming."

"I'll bet you say that to all the girls," I said, expecting a ready denial and further flattery.

But he replied: "I do."

Now if, at the conclusion of our encounter, I'd kissed *his* hand ("Thank you so much for seeing me, Mr. Montalban") and he'd said, "You are very charming," I might have had the parting shot (emboldened by my hand-kissing initiative) with, "That's what all the boys say."

Surprise moves are disconcerting, so it's doubtful that Mr. Montalban would have come up with a snappy riposte. But it isn't *only* to get the upper hand that one should wish to kiss it, although *I* would see that as its primary function, whether it's used in a sexual, social, or professional way.

I know a lot of women would rather slap a hand than kiss it — but that habit, although it has reached beyond color, is stubbornly bro to bro and shows little sign of reaching beyond gender.

Neither has hand kissing, you may say, arguing that it has reached beyond class, but not beyond gender. True. But there is no reason why it couldn't, and we women could find ourselves using it with skill and profit before men (given the prejudice most have against it) realized its value. Shouldn't we give it a whirl?

Practice will be necessary if it is to be done smoothly. Rather than risk the ridicule of friends and relatives, I've been using the paw of a cat. Dogs are out since they are — at least the ones I know — pathetically eager for affection and would give me an inflated idea of my performance. Cats, on the other hand, are touchy, and if they think they're being used will react to a kiss on the paw with a scratch on the nose. So far I have been able to plant a variety of kisses with only a scratch or two, which indicates that I've been successful at disguising the motive that prompted them. It won't be long before I am ready for the real thing.

I have already selected the first recipient, and if you hear a man say: "So what I renewed her lease indefinitely with no rent increase. You wanna know why?" — and here his voice will break and he'll choke back a sob — ". . . because its the first time in my goddammed life anyone ever treated me like a gentleman" — you'll know it's working.

Type A Personality in a
Type F World

As I write this I am reading Cecil Beaton's diaries (*The Strenuous Years* — 1948–1955), recording Ella off the radio, checking Jimmy Breslin's column, soaking my underwear in the sink, eating and drinking, sighing and coughing, laughing and crying, scratching and stretching, and slapping the cat.

I believe that life is too short to do one thing at a time and that the future belongs to those who can make love, write novels, and recover from the flu while taking violin lessons.

But it does not belong to me, because although I am a Type A personality, I am, tragically, in a Type F world.

Bitterly, I reflect (as I pluck my eyebrows, stir the soup, and floss my teeth) on Donna Karan, who is a Type A personality in a Type A world. Even as Donna rides in her limo, she gets a pedicure, sketches her next collection, watches the *Today* show, does her face-stretching exercises, and arrives at her studio ready to make executive decisions, check

41

production, learn Japanese, lunch (a gauzy slice or two of cucumber, a demishrimp), and have her hips resculpted by her personal masseuse.

How much easier life would be if I were in a Type A world and I had help in maintaining that furious pace.

But I must go it alone. Unlike Donald Trump, I have no one urging me on. No one is revving up my helicopter, no one is clamoring for me to sign the contract, no one is eager to negotiate the deal, no group waits for me to take meetings, throw parties, throw fits, ruin competitors, overthrow governments.

Bearing up under discouragement that would fell a Rupert Murdoch (who I can match, second for second, in multilayered activity), I go on. I'd like to see how long *he'd* last if he had to put up with ugly rejection on every side as I do. I'd like to see how long *he'd* run with the fast crowd if there weren't the continual encouragement of *more* newspapers, *more* TV stations for him to play with.

I'd like to see him put up with the derision I get. "Oh my, we *are* busy," my friends say. Or, in the case of one offensive French person, *"Où est le feu?"*

Like any Type A personality, I don't let my life stop because I happen to find myself on the street. Yet does Bob Pittman — president of Quantum Media, which produced *The Morton Downey, Jr., Show* — have to suffer the ridicule of strangers as he dresses down a subordinate on Madison Avenue, as I do for giving an editor a piece of my mind on the very same spot? Just because he's talking into a portable phone and I appear to be talking to myself?

Let's face it: in a Type A world, you have the facilities to be a Type A personality with *dignity.* But although I must do without them, I will never change. Because to me, doing,

doing, doing is as natural as breathing, even though I come from a family of sluggards and my mother couldn't listen to the radio and boil potatoes at the same time.

And I wonder if Rupert or Donald or *any* of them are *natural* Type A's. Could it be that they have simply been forced by circumstances to adjust their speed to their surroundings?

Well, it's a sobering thought, and almost enough to give me pause — except that it is not something I can fit into my fast-paced life. Frankly, I don't have a millisecond to spare to reflect on the tragedy of a Type F personality trapped in a Type A world.

I Grew My Nails and It Changed My Life

I had always lived with nails that begged to be ignored. So, at first, I didn't realize what was happening; it wasn't anything deliberate. It happened when I switched from a masochistic manual typewriter that demanded all the pounding I could give it, to a well-balanced electric model that asked only a feather-light touch. One day I noticed that my nails, which had always been shorter than my fingers, were jutting out beyond them. I was astonished, because although I had occasionally produced a long nail on the odd finger or thumb, I have never possessed an entire set of nails capable of steady, uniform growth. It was thrilling. But how long would it continue if they weren't given some kind of encouragement? Even if my work no longer posed a threat (and even here a nervous chat with an editor could bring on a fit of nibbling), everything else in my life did. When you have no nails to speak of, you are not in the habit of protecting them. Suddenly anything — peeling an orange, combing your hair, nagging a child — could cause a break.

My first step was to consult a friend in the beauty business. She got me a special hardener, which she told me was banned in the States (I was living in Montreal then) because it was used as an embalming fluid. It certainly mummified my nails, and also kept me in such a state of fright, lest it petrify the rest of me, that my hands were never near my mouth. What went into it instead was a ginseng root, which was all the rage ten years ago as a magical elixir. Already, I thought, as I chewed away on the root instead of my nails, I am protecting myself from disease and prolonging my life.

A week of conscious nail growing forced me to ask myself if nail neglect had prevented me from achieving a fully realized life. It is said that the Chinese grew their nails for status, to show they didn't need to use their hands, but could there have been more to it than that? Could their nails have provided a focus, a meaning, a direction? Would mine? Or would they mark me as rapacious, cold, scheming, frivolous? Would they cause me to be left out when the conversation got serious? Would I find myself pursued by persons with unsettling sexual requirements? There was only one way to find out. Keep growing them and see.

From then on I became obsessed with my nails. I drank gelatin, soaked my hands in soapy water, prodded my cuticles, and shyly painted my nails pale pink until one day I felt they were long enough for crimson. Rarely have I seen a lovelier sight.

I took my nails over to the typewriter and rested them on the keys. But as they lay there, I realized they looked wrong. They did not look, as I hoped they would, like literary nails. They looked like the nails any office worker might have grown purely for adornment, with no larger purpose in mind. Yet away from the typewriter, they became executive nails that got someone else to do the typing for them. Could I keep my nails and continue in my profession? Perhaps if I painted them a socially undesirable shade? So I gave myself navy nails and embarrassed my children, who saw the move as a misguided attempt at punk chic: "Mom, you are too old for your nails," they said.

And, in any shade, my nails insulted the dishevelment of my lover. When I had mediocre nails, his untidiness had some dignity. Against my new nails, he merely looked grubby. I told him it was better if we didn't see each other anymore.

Getting rid of him was one thing. I still had to live with my house, which I had always thought had a certain bookish dash; now, compared to my nails, it reminded me of a Russian trying to look hip.

The point was that I had magnificent nails. Nails that put me in the same class as Cher, Barbra Streisand, and Gloria Steinem. The difference between us, however, was that they lived up to their nails, while I could not. My nails only succeeded in showing me how inferior the rest of my life was.

I knew that I could not live with them, and that if I ignored them, they would just go away. But I determined to exercise control to the last, and so I decided to cut them. Once I'd made the decision, I hung on a couple of weeks longer because I wanted to show them off when I interviewed Gene Wilder. But if he noticed my nails, he said nothing. I felt let down, even though I knew nails like mine were commonplace in his show biz world, and that, in fact, dirty, ragged, bitten, disgusting nails were more likely to excite his attention.

The day after the interview, I ceremoniously painted them one last time and then cut them. I thought of keeping the tips as one keeps a lock of hair. Perhaps my daughters would carry these relics in a locket as a memento of what Mother might have been.

Occasionally, I have regretted that I didn't persevere. But, if anything, I think long nails would have dulled my ambition. Knowing that perfection was always possible with them, I would have let everything else slide.

Is this happening to my teenage daughter Sophie? She had developed extraordinary nails — modeling them on the set she saw on Ali MacGraw when she sat next to her at Shakespeare in the Park — and every week she travels all the way to SoHo from the Upper West Side to have them tended.

"Only Annie understands my nails," she says.

I fear Sophie could, as I would, look upon her nails as an end in themselves — unlike my friend Diane. When she found it increasingly difficult to hold her tongue or disguise her contempt for her corporate colleagues, she looked to her nails for help. She began to spend her lunch hours patronizing those nail salons where Korean girls wrap breaks in silk. Soon Diane had beautiful, long nails, which she studied in business meetings, appearing to be lost in contemplation. Actually, she was using them to calm her feelings of annoyance and focus her mind on matters of *real* consequence. Her nails taught her to be cool, and since growing them, she has been wooed away by a rival concern.

I don't doubt that many others have had their lives changed by growing their nails. Perhaps we will start to see testimonials in those nail salons that seem to be springing up everywhere. Perhaps manicurists will become as important as they were in the early 1900s, when they outranked hairdressers. Then, as now, the field was dominated by women, with men barred from the trade because of the need to hold the customer's hand. If manicuring once again assumes great importance, perhaps it will attract them. Surely a job that offers the chance to hold hands (if only for the grooming of nails) is not to be lightly dismissed in this lonely and uneasy world?

I have never had a manicure myself. Even during that brief period when I had glorious nails, I couldn't bring myself to seek professional help. But that experience left me with an interest in doing my own nails, or at least painting them whatever their condition. Right now they're sporting a couple of coats of L'Oreal's Butternut.

The sight of them pleases me because they look like the nails of my Jewish aunties who, with their henna'd hair, cigarettes, high heels, and sexy tailor-mades spelled glamour to me as a child. Even though their nails showed the wear and tear of working in a garment factory, they were painted Tropic Orange. They would no more deny their nails this decorative touch than they would dream of leaving off their lipstick.

Their nails and mine say the same thing: We're working women, but we like to doll up. These are nails I can live with, and, who knows, maybe even grow by.

To Garrote a Carrot

When I was first married, I got a gadget that was supposed to chop parsley as finely as grains of sand. It did if I put the effort into it, but to me a gadget is useful only if it saves labor or eliminates it altogether.

So the parsley chopper was put in a drawer with carrot dicers and cabbage shredders and tomato slicers and hamburger molders and egg decapitators, where it remains to this day.

Every so often, one of my children will pick up one of these gadgets and say, "What's this?" Then there is a brief moment of mystery until I remember it is a mushroom fluter.

I've had my flings with popcorn makers, waffle irons, and Crockpots. I was wild about a double-bladed electric carving knife that produced gossamer slices once and never worked properly again. I put on ten pounds during my affair with an automatic french-fryer. But now they all stand abandoned, like the discarded lovers they are, in my cupboard.

I once thought a rotisserie could change my life. And it would have, but I never mastered the art of trussing and strapping a chicken to the spit. I would go off and leave the bird to twirl, but after a few spins, the limbs would dangle loose and a jutting leg would act like a brake, causing the spit to jam. And when I went to serve dinner, I would find the main course burned on one side and raw on the other.

Once you own a gadget, you feel guilty if you don't use it. I got so sick of sneaking ready-made spaghetti past the pasta machine that I gave the thing to my daughter. I knew it wouldn't bother her to flaunt store-bought stuff in front of it. How often have I snatched an orange from her, crying: "How dare you eat that when I have a juice extractor?"

I have two gadgets, though, that are always indulged — the coffee grinder and the food processor.

I was deeply infatuated with the food processor from the first. I loved the way it bossed food around. The way it blended soups that once took days of cooking to get the same flavor. The way it *dealt* with garlic. When I first had it, I could deny it nothing. It was fed whole meals to puree.

"Can't I eat like a grown man," my ex-husband would whine, "instead of a nine-month-old baby?"

My excessive use of the food processor may have been brought on by an unhappy marriage. Certainly, since the divorce, the machine and I have settled down to a steady relationship of soups, sauces, and salad dressings. I haven't tried to puree a lamb chop in it since my husband left.

As a matter of fact, I am thinking of reviving some other relationships. I've been giving the Crockpot the eye lately. I dream of him greeting me on a wintry night with the fragrance of slow-cooking stew. I'm getting a VCR from the kids for my birthday and intend to groom the popcorn maker as my movie date.

I'll bet there are women like me all over America who lost their husbands but found their waffle irons. I think a study should be done (*Household Gadgets and the Divorcée*, perhaps) examining the significance of this phenomenon. And I say this because for the first time in years, I find myself ready to use that parsley chopper again. I was always very competitive with my husband; now I realize I am competing with the food processor.

If there were a study of the sort I have suggested, at least I could find out if this is a sign of progress or not.

Under Writers — Lingerie and the Literati

Did Gertrude Stein wear boxer shorts? We assume she did, but she never spoke of it. Or perhaps she did and nobody understood what she was saying. I have checked the diaries and letters but can find no word as to whether Virginia Woolf switched when cami knickers cast out old-style bloomers. As a founding member of the Bloomsbury group, she may have stayed with the latter purely for their name's sake.

I would not be thinking about this except that I have just taken off a pair of panty hose that were driving me mad because the crotch refused to budge much past the knee. I tried to work (doing a piece on jock chic, as a matter of fact), hoping my exertions would stretch them to fit. But they hobbled me physically and mentally, and as I was removing them, I got to wondering if other writers were affected by their underwear.

Would Gertrude or Virginia have been happy with panty hose? I can tell you Harold Pinter (who may or may not wear Y-fronts) wasn't. When they were first introduced, he denounced them for reducing to a featureless zone what had been an area sexily cluttered with a busy complex of stocking tops, garter belts, and lace panties.

Harold's idea that torso and limb should be treated separately, like church and state, found little support among women. I thought it was a contemptible macho statement and joined the millions of others who bought panty hose to the exclusion of everything else, causing a drastic decline in girdle and lingerie sales. "Awfullest in the Underworld," one hard-hit corset man declared of the offending tights.

And then Madonna came along. There are many who do not believe that she deserves her sacred name, but believe me, the girdle and lingerie interests aren't among them. They are eternally grateful to Our Lady of the Two-Way Stretch for breaking the monopolistic hold the pornographers had on our stocking tops, garters, and all the other saucy stuff meant for universal consumption. And women everywhere owe Madonna their prayers of thanks for giving them the right to roller-skate in the corselette.

Colette would have loved it. As it was, she flashed her corseted torso and cheeky thighs to music hall audiences and hung out, *chez elle*, in stays and chemise or, adapting her lingerie for the ladies among her lovers, in something boyish. She would certainly have agreed with Cole Porter (I see *him* in custom-cut shorts, sharply creased and debonair), who wrote in the musical *Silk Stockings:*

> *Strange what undergarments do*
> *To convert a maiden's point of view*

— a hint that it was satin next to the skin (after those rough Bolshevik bloomers) that caused his heroine, Ninotchka, to defect.

"I dreamed I became a capitalist playgirl in my Maiden-form bra . . . ," Ninotchka might have said, echoing that famous ad campaign from the fifties, when *Silk Stockings* was released. Maidenform bras, those hoary ads stressed, fitted a girl for anything in life; "I dreamed . . ." took in the gondola ride, the mountain climb, the visit to the opera, and so on. The campaign also slyly awoke erotic fantasies among us girls about being half-dressed in a public place (through no fault of our own).

If only the world could see how seductive we were under our meek office blouses! Underneath we'd be revealed, voluptuous *and* commanding, in our shiny-satin, 36B-cup, seamed-like-Wonder-Woman's breastplates: "I dreamed I *gave* dictation in my Maidenform bra . . . ," we'd proudly proclaim.

The campaign contradicted everything my mother had warned me to expect if exposed in public in provocative underwear that included the uplift bra. She and the medical profession stood as one, she was confident, in holding that such fripperies inflamed the already ungovernable lusts of men, offered no protection against pneumonia, and disqualified you for treatment if you were hit by a bus.

Mother would have renamed the campaign "I dreamed I had an accident . . ." and run ads depicting a surgeon so profoundly disgusted by the sluttish black-lace bra that he would refuse to operate: "This harlot is not worth saving," he would say, snapping his scalpel shut and leaving the Maidenform model to expire on the operating table.

Other mothers believed it was the condition (shabby, grubby) of their daughter's underwear that would excite such loathing. A friend of mine brought up with this point of view thought it might help her when she was helplessly drawn to a Eurotrash cad, and she deliberately wore *stale* underwear to an assignation with him hoping the shame of exposure would deter her from jumping into bed. It did no such thing. She forgot about it completely. It was only afterward, when Pierre — with insufferable Gallic superiority — held up her soup-stained teddy with an expression of distaste and inquired, "You eat your dinnair in zees?" that she remembered why she'd worn it in the first place.

Mother always thought the French behaved badly around underwear and held them responsible for inventing the lust-inciting kind in the first place. *Risqué* was the word she used to describe it — only she pronounced it "risk," something her dishabille never exposed her to. Her's was so totally without allure it could be exposed on the seaside outing if the weather turned warm. Removing her blouse, she would let the sun shine in on a bodice layered with enough vests, bras, and slips to distribute up to three or four sets of straps at each shoulder.

In a way, Mother was the forerunner of that later fashion of exposed shoulder-straps to which Madonna has lent such seductive nonchalance. I only wish the Material Girl had been around when I was a teenager wearing my Merry Widow corselette. That would have licensed me to expose it on the dance floor so the boy I was waltzing with could see how seductive it *looked,* not just how impregnable it *felt* as the jutting apparatus of its wired bra prevented us from dancing close.

Still, it did cinch my waist to a size I never achieved through diet and exercise — though it also had Mother darkly predicting that for such vanity I was ruining my kidneys and my chances of bearing children.

Mother is the only woman I have ever known to wear a

roomy corset. Far from contouring her shape, it simply provided a scaffold on which to hang her clothes. Anyway, she said she didn't feel dressed without it.

Sometimes, I feel I could use a little whalebone in my life — not to flatten my stomach, but to stiffen my resolve; not to shape my body, but my purpose. It would be buckled on much like a suit of armor and would be just the impetus I need to dash off the major work.

And while it is possible that Gertrude Stein's underwear (or Virginia Woolf's, for that matter) had absolutely nothing to do with their genius as writers, I believe, in my own case, mine could be the very basis of my work.

I can see future critics and analysts puzzled that a mind that had always seemed as formless as my own could suddenly begin to manifest itself (in plays, novels, whatever) with such depth, such breadth, such *structure*.

At a loss, they will cast about for someone to call in to solve the mystery. I suggest Madonna. "Look to her corset," she will say. "Roomy enough for freedom of expression, yet in its restraint reminding her of the importance of discipline."

The mystery solved, critics will not be slow in seeing the possibilities elsewhere. If Madonna, having introduced the area of investigation, declines to pursue it further, perhaps Harold Pinter, who has already shown an aptitude for looking into ladies' lingerie, will address himself to the specifically literary.

In getting to the bottom, you can be sure, he will start at the top with Jane Austen and address the mystery of why, although she was a spinster, no hint of repression can be found in her work. After months of investigation, Mr. Pinter will reveal that it was lint — a substance regarded as mildly stimulating when trapped in the knickers — that gave Jane the modest carnal relief that was more than sufficient to give her the balanced attitude that makes her novels masterpieces.

Perhaps in the future there'll be a bookish chant that will go:

> *The man who gave us the Pinter pause*
> *Revealed the secret of Jane Austen's drawers.*

There should be.

Oh, THAT Cosmo Girl

I was never a volunteer anything. Who had the time! If you want a career you have to put in the hours. If you happen to be husband-hunting you have to slosh around in the social jungle. How much can one person do! Find the time, my favorite magazine said. You're needed, you won't be so self-involved and your life will be enriched. So here I am every Tuesday night in the soup kitchen, making sandwiches. I think I am a better person. I know I am a happier one. I love that magazine. I guess you could say I'm That COSMOPOLITAN GIRL.

— Ad from the *New York Times*

Articles

• You've brought the paillards, the radicchio, the *fraises*, the Evian water. You're barefoot in the park with dinner *à deux* to go! You're dining alfresco! It's fun, it's different, it's romantic! You've solved the man shortage! You're DATING THE HOMELESS.

• When doing good turns bad — confessions of a compulsive volunteer. "I'd take on anything. Meals on Wheels. Anything. My career suffered. I gained weight. I lost my boyfriend, my pores were clogged, I broke a nail." I'M JUST A GAL WHO CAN'T SAY NO.

• Can you be *against* wasteful welfare spending, but *for* the poor? Yes! Handouts and help from the private sector are what it's all about! *Cosmo* talks to Missy van Belk, beautiful young Republican, who helps welfare families, seniors, and the disabled *without* compromising her principles! SISTER! YOU CAN SHARE A DIME.

• The stars expose the secrets behind their concern for incest, battered wives, famine, drug abuse, animal abuse, etc., etc. Learn who cares about what . . . and why! You may be surprised! THOSE VERY(!) PERSONAL CRUSADES.

PLUS

Fashion

SOUP KITCHEN SPANDEX! Top model ZuZu raises morale ("I felt like Marilyn Monroe entertaining the GIs") dishing out the soup in this season's sexiest, most sizzling styles.

Diet

"Mother used to make me finish meals because of the starving children. Now the starving children finish them!" Staying slim with food giveaways! LOSING POUNDS ON MORAL GROUNDS.

Beauty

Devoting yourself to others can be hard on hair, skin, nails. Don't miss our BEAUTY TIPS FOR GOOD SAMARITANS.

Exercise

REACH OUT! And Up! And Over! Astounding new stretching program.

Horoscope

Is the War on Want really *you?* Choose a charity to match your sign. This month: CANCER CAUSES.

SPECIAL BONUS OFFER!

Clean out your closet and pack discards-to-donate in this smart, vinyl tote wittily embossed BAG LADY. Only $9.95.

ON YOUR NEWSSTANDS SOON!

You Can Never Be Too Rich
or Too Relaxed

. . . he is completely relaxed with the notion of being rich, with the phenomenon of instant wealth, with conspicuous consumption.

— Michael Korda, editor in chief of Simon and Schuster,
describing John Fairchild, publisher of *M, W,* and
Women's Wear Daily and author of *Chic Savages,*
a nonfiction account of nouvelle society for which
Simon and Schuster paid a million dollars
(as quoted by Suzy in the *New York Post*)

Why is John Fairchild *completely relaxed* about being rich? Are you telling me his money never makes him tense up? The answer is Yes! because John Fairchild reigns over that part of nouvelle society which not only dresses society but *is* society.

I speak of those dressmakers, those interior decorators, those hairdressers who suffered *centuries* of humiliation, insults, and tantrums from duchesses and dictators, magnates and heiresses, but who are now the privileged elite themselves! And because they *are* the tastemakers and trendsetters, they never suffer from that edginess (which has so often afflicted the upper crust) about how they *spend* their money. And isn't that, after all, the point of being rich?

In the past, while robber barons, inbred royals, and schizoid heiresses might be *completely relaxed* about their ability to make, extort, steal, and inherit money, they were often uptight when it came to spending it.

It has been thought that self-consciousness about displaying wealth stems from an embarrassment about how it is made. A more likely explanation, I believe, is an unsureness of taste. In other words, you cannot be *completely relaxed* about spending the money you made as a munitions magnate, say, if you suspect the world is laughing at your hat.

Of course, you can hire a millinery adviser, but if you have no confidence in your taste, you will never be *completely relaxed* about your choice of consultant.

There is plenty of evidence to show us that there are many among the wealthy who are not, by the standards of nouvelle society, *completely relaxed* with being rich. In a spirit of defiance, many have been pointlessly extravagant (spending millions on such useless acquisitions as eighteenth-century English landscapes); others have *fussed* (endowing, bequeathing, donating, funding) hoping attention would be distracted from their lack of taste by these disbursements; still others (fearful of inviting derision every time they spend a buck) have stashed away their money and lived like paupers.

Now the moneyed fashion elite displays no such reticence. They have the taste (why wouldn't they? — they make it) and they *want* to show it off because they are *completely relaxed* about being rich (unlike free-spending art collectors and misguided philanthropists).

All right, then — is there *nothing* that shakes that carefree attitude of nouvelle society? Even the fact that they are nouveau riche? Because haven't the nouveau always lived in dread of being dismissed by the *ancien*? Isn't that flicker of fear that often mars Nancy Reagan's expression caused by this? Undeniably — but remember, Nancy is not a tastemaker; she relies on the tastemakers. There will always be moments when Nancy is shaken by doubt — are those beaded sheath gowns an unforgettable statement or merely monotonous? — which is why she cannot feel *completely relaxed* about being rich.

But Bill Blass, who created those gowns, is totally at ease now that he is at the very center of that society he could only have hoped to serve before. And the money that has made that possible has come to him through *licensing* — in other words, his powers as tastemaker are the very source of his fortune. As the bucks blow in from Blass sheets and Blass shirts, naturally Bill is happy to spend them on high-profile items like stretch limos and lunch at Le Cygne with "his gals" Nancy Kissinger, Nan Kempner, Judy Peabody, Pat Buckley.

But are there never moments of nervousness? Never a time, just when Judy is telling him (as she told *W*) that he is as sophisticated and charming "as a Cole Porter song" and he is feeling completely relaxed, that he spots John Fairchild across the room? And do their eyes meet and is Bill seized by an icy chill? And do his cuff links suddenly look gauche?

It is nightmarish to contemplate, but should that look ever alight on Bill, it would be enough for him to realize he would never again be *completely relaxed* about being rich. Only John Fairchild, maker and breaker of tastemakers, can afford to be that.

Getting the Bold Shoulder

"Pull those shoulders back!" my gym teacher Miss Cream would bark, in a vain attempt to get me to straighten up from my fashionable slouch.

I considered her ideas on posture (and indeed of gymnastics generally) as a primitive and inefficient means of figure loveliness for the modern miss.

"Girdles and bras can give us a better shape than any amount of exercising," I declared. "Anyway," I said, "who wants to look like Joan Crawford?"

I certainly didn't, but under Miss Cream's coaching the risk was considerable. My shoulders were already bigger than those of the weedy boys who were attracted to me. Perhaps they saw in my well-developed shoulders the sexual maturity they lacked. Anyway, the New Look was in and it was *my* shoulders that were meant to be narrow, sloping, and unobtrusive.

Instead they were square — not only totally wrong for the New Look, but reminiscent of the old-fashioned, out-of-date, deeply vulgar wartime one of wedgies, upsweeps, and boxy suits. In 1947, when a fashion was out it was out (not like now, when we can hardly wait for a style to go out so we can bring it back in again) and we despised anything that wasn't *current*.

This was the postwar world. Paris, silenced under the Occupation, once again dictated fashion. The natural order had been restored. Pushy, assertive shoulders like mine were completely out of place on the contemporary woman with her tiny, cinched-in waist and her petticoats to the ankles.

Even after the New Look was the old look and people said that if it were only a question of shoulders, Grace Kelly and I would be look-alikes, I still hated my shoulders. As far as I was concerned, Grace's major flaw was that she had the face of the fifties set on the shoulders of the forties.

Fashions came and went, hems rose and fell, breasts were in and out, but nothing sufficiently significant happened to shoulders to move me from my conviction that the narrower they were, the better. As routinely as others got their hems altered, I had my sleeves set in from the armholes.

"But that's two inches in from the edge of your shoulder," dressmakers would protest.

"Good," I would say. "The closer to the neck, the better."

I kept this up for years until exercising became the fashion rage and I discovered that, in a leotard, it was only the squareness of my shoulders that saved me from flabby disaster. My chief figure fault had become my major asset!

Now not only did I fling my shoulders back, I flaunted them. Where once I would stop at nothing to minimize them, now they could not be big enough. When shoulder pads were revived and I realized that, if they were big enough, I had a waist by comparison, it was like discovering that high-heeled shoes make your legs look longer.

It was over the shoulder line now, with pads going into everything I owned. The limp rags in my closet seemed to spring to life. And I felt what Joan Crawford must have experienced when Adrian first put pads in her costumes for *Letty Lynton,* in 1932, to stop them from drooping.

Naturally, I thought of how different my life would have been if Schiaparelli (who had introduced "shelf" shoulders in the thirties) had been the fashion force in 1947 rather than Christian Dior. Who knows what heights I might have achieved as I shouldered my way to the top? When I think of how I'd even refused to shrug my shoulders for fear of drawing attention to them! Now, having discovered that one pound of shoulder pads could wipe out ten pounds of fat, my shoulders were as flagrant as Joan Crawford's.

"Her and her damned shoulder pads," said film director Michael Curtiz when he rejected Joan for *Mildred Pierce.* But she got the role anyway. And, playing it with her shoulders at their most extravagant — and her mouth and eyebrows made up to match — she won an Oscar.

Joan used her shoulders (as men do) for power and authority, as well as for creative expression. Things might have been a whole lot different if, instead of deriding her back in the forties, I had done the same. Was it too late to do it now? I tried writing with my Mike Tyson pads stuffed into my bathrobe. I did develop a certain belligerence — perhaps because the pads were hot and made me irritable — but never reached that state of determined bellicosity needed to KO Iris Murdoch. So, unlike Joan, who would have stood by her pads no matter what, I gave them up as working tools.

Soon shoulder pads were to play no part in my life at all. I had given up dieting when I found out how effective they were in creating the illusion of a waist. Now even the largest weren't equal to the task.

For the past couple of years, I have been trying to become reconciled to my shoulders. I made this decision after I took a yoga class and the instructor urged us to knead our knees and thank them daily for the vital role they play in our lives. She told us the story of a woman who had always knocked her knees because they were continually giving way under her, but once she started acknowledging their importance on a daily basis, they never gave her another moment's trouble.

Hearing this, I began to feel uneasy about my shoulders. I didn't have much to thank them for, but maybe I should do it anyway. A while back, I felt a twinge in one of them and my friend said it sounded like tennis shoulder. I don't even play tennis. So I have taken to massaging my shoulders and having a word or two. Crossing my arms and clutching them, I will tell them that what we have to do now is learn to live and work together for our mutual benefit. True, this hasn't happened so far, but, hey, I'm prepared to shoulder part of the blame for that. The important thing to remember is what's past is past and there's no sense whatsoever in flaring up now over old grievances.

I just hope the message is getting through.

That's Evolution!

Has John Cleese been tested for steroids? When we saw him naked in *A Fish Called Wanda*, we gasped. Basil Fawlty with biceps! He *said* he worked out with a personal trainer. But we know he's having hair transplants and so therefore is not philosophically opposed to augmentation. And anyway, could he lift weights without giggling? No, my guess is steroids. I see their use spreading among other comics — not only to Steve, Dan, Tom, and Robin, but to Pee-wee and to Martin Short, ending forever the classic shtick of the ninety-pound weakling. Even Woody, the most serious of our funnymen, has undoubtedly asked: "Where in the Torah does it say that a man shouldn't be entitled to a little definition?"

Where indeed. I see nothing wrong with enhancement, with augmentation. Isn't that what it's all about? And as with athletes, comics too will be capable of undreamed-of comic feats, such as multiple pratfalls or an incredibly rapid delivery rate of one-liners.

It's a disgrace, I think, that they took Ben Johnson's Olympic medal from him. Would the Oscar have been snatched from Cher if it was found she had taken the odd silicone injection to ensure the even greater perfection of that extraordinarily conditioned flesh? Would the Academy have determined that she had had an unfair advantage over the other contenders? Of course not.

And while the subject is silicone —

"Read my lips!" you heard George Bush say, but what you didn't hear was the man who called out, "What lips?" But some did hear. And some thought about lips — lips that would not need to *mouth* anything, lips that would be expressive in and of themselves. Donald Trump's enemies are calling him sili-lips, but even they can't deny that his genius for negotiation is greater now that he can pout.

And if it's true that Donald has rubber lips, why hide it? Mariel Hemingway told the world she got sili-boobs to play Dorothy Stratton. Not just to look but to *be* the part. Silicone, like steroids, *creating* art. Has Sylvester Stallone been up-front with us? Is Rambo's build due to only the gym and the effort of rubbing out Commie freaks in his movies or was there the odd injection? C'mon, Sly, give credit where credit's due.

The National Football League has been testing its players. Positive results are not rampant, but according to Mark Murphy, who used to play for the Washington Redskins, that's because the tests are given only once, at the start of the season; the players know they're coming, so they have time to clear their systems. How awful that we should require such deception by our fine young athletes, who seek only to satisfy the fans' and the owners' *demand* for bigger and stronger players — even though steroids could cause

70

cancer (which they surely do — because, hey, *everything* causes cancer).

The bottom line is that the players take steroids because they want to be the best they can be. That is all any kind of player wants, whether we speak of Woody or Sly, Pee-wee or Donald. Or rather, they want more. They want to be better than anybody in their field has ever been in the history of man. And that, to me, is evolution — and nobody ever said that had to be 100-percent natural, now did they?

Seconds

As someone who was a second wife, I am deeply envious of the way Nancy Reagan was treated in the First Family feud. Ron said he agonized over the way his son Michael upset Nancy by publicly complaining that she had never seen her stepgrandchild.

Boy, I wish I'd been married to Ron. My ex-husband had nothing to say but shape up or ship out when I objected to the pets my stepdaughter brought over and left at our house. My husband pointed out to me that he had discussed the matter thoroughly with his first wife and both had agreed that children from broken homes need pets. Since her place had just been redecorated, it was thought the pets should be kept at our house. Now, can you imagine Ron consulting Jane Wyman and landing Nancy with something like that?

I wouldn't have minded, but no pet my stepdaughter ever brought us on her weekend visits was what I'd call in mint condition. She was keen on castoffs. We got sluggish fish swimming in bowls of toxic waste, a moth-eaten canary called Bob in a rusty cage, and a vicious cat named Lewis.

Because the fish soon succumbed to their surroundings, my husband thought Bob's chance of survival would be improved if he had nicer living conditions, so he built him an elaborately carved balsa cage. Before you could say "Pretty Boy," Bob had pecked his way out of this fretted paradise and Lewis ate him. Naturally, I was blamed. I had often voiced my dislike of the pair and, undoubtedly, stood by doing nothing when the tragedy occurred.

"You're a wicked stepmother, Mom," my *own* children cried. Was this charge ever leveled at Nancy by Patty or Ron Jr. over Michael's baby? Honestly, I doubt it.

Nancy's stepdaughter Maureen even acts as family hatchet person and calls Michael names to spare Nancy the indignity.

Of course, Maureen may hope to become Daddy's little girl (at last!) by getting to him through Nancy. My daughters (step or natural) would never try such a thing since, if anything, an alliance formed with me would rule them out from their father's favor.

It may have escaped Ron's notice that he actually has kids; he and Nancy are just so profoundly *nuclear* — it's always just the two of them. But even now that the couple has posed for a photograph with the group, I wouldn't be surprised if Ron, seeing the picture sometime in the future, said: "You look great, Nancy. Who was the supporting cast?"

I can't help comparing the picture of the Reagans with one of my family. The children are clustered around my ex and another Nancy (in this case a despicable dalmatian owned by my stepdaughter). I'm not even in the shot. And if you think it's petty of me to dwell on it, let me only say, that was our Christmas card that year.

Trying On

I am a clothes-mad person whose wardrobe would be three times the size it is if I didn't have to try things on.

I have a fitting-room phobia. And is it any wonder? I enter with the simple desire to find out if the maillot swimsuit is for me and I exit not only knowing it is not, but with a lot of other information I can live without.

I might be hardened to such experiences if I had been brought up to try things on. But I was not. In wartime England, my mother always selected clothing several sizes too large that I would "grow into." I never met her expectations. By the time I fit them, they weren't fit to be worn.

Deprived of the chance to try on my own things for size, let alone style, I tried on mother's instead.

I remember putting on her plum velvet evening gown and buckling my five-year-old brother into her corset as a suit of armor, so he could play Lancelot to my Guinevere.

Mother, surprising us at this charade, found the sight of my brother so deeply shocking that I escaped punishment.

74

Instead, hasty family conferences were called, and he was suddenly given the football boots he wasn't expecting until his birthday.

I thought of this incident when I was back on a visit to London and in one of those boutiques with wide-open changing spaces.

The only other occupant in the changing room I'll call Ms. Crotchpatch, since that's all she was wearing. Languidly, she smoked a cigarette and watched as I fumbled my way out of my clothes, revealing underpants to the waist and a bra long on sturdiness and short on allure.

Crotchpatch was waiting for her friend who was scouting the racks and returning every so often with possibilities.

"Do you fancy lime taffeta with seed pearls, ducky?"

"No, I don't," Crotchpatch pouted. "You're supposed to be looking for something for me, not yourself, Nigel."

Certainly, with his Boy George dreadlocks, smock, and platform shoes, it wasn't an unreasonable accusation. Still, Nigel seemed eager to please. Catching sight of me sizing myself up in the factory overalls debs were said to disco in, he asked: "Where you off to then? The night shift?"

"I heard Princess Di thinks they're amusing," I said, trying to make light of matters.

"Amusing, love. Not laughable. Come on, you don't want to look like the lady foreman. There's a sequined tent out there. Fit any size, it would. Want me to bring it in?"

I didn't want anyone looking for clothes for me who sounded so much like my mother, so I declined.

I don't always come off so badly in open fitting rooms. In fact, at the discount houses in the United States, where they have dispensed with partitions not in a spirit of permissiveness but to pass the savings on to us, I am apt to shine.

On my last visit, I certainly felt superior to the woman next to me who had discarded her down jacket, pilled sweater, and jeans to try on a ruffled dress in flamingo pink. Finding it difficult to judge its effectiveness with her sneakers on, she sought my opinion.

"Does this do anything for me?"

It brought out a greenish tinge to her skin and made her look fifteen pounds heavier, but if this wasn't apparent to her, why not look for a positive aspect?

"It could be an Oscar de la Renta."

"Is that right — and it's only thirty-nine ninety-five!"

Thrilled by the magic of the name, if not by her own appearance, she decided to buy the dress.

"Are you getting that?" she asked of the new, longer-length, slender-line coat I was trying on. I'd seen it advertised for $450. Here, it was $150.

"I might," I said.

"Is it for winter?"

"Of course." How could I expect a woman with so little fashion savvy to know what season it was for?

"Then you ought to get a size you can button up," she said.

At these savings, you don't get size selection. I decided to buy it anyway, going for the dash of the open coat and praying we would have a mild winter.

Even when I am prepared to pay full price, I run into trouble.

"Am I that guerrilla girl?" I ask myself as militaristic models swagger into view on the video in the department store. I could be. Everything looks so roomy.

I select a jacket, two pairs of multipocketed pants (to give myself the size choice), a shirt, and a T-shirt with Chinese characters on it that probably say "Down with American Imperialist Running Dogs."

"Only five to a customer," the wardress in charge of the fitting cells barks. Smugly, I indicate to her that I have not exceeded my quota. She subtracts the T-shirt anyway, claiming it is from JAPS (three racks away) and not to be tried on in La Vie Denime, which is where I am now standing.

The cell she assigns me is lit as savagely as any prison. I look like a terrorist even before I try on the clothes. Once I am in them, it is not fresh, young fashion rebel who confronts me in the glass, but battle-worn veteran.

Just the same, I might take them — except the price of terrorist chic is too high for me to take a chance on them looking okay once the lighting is right. Corporate clothes that sing the praises of capitalism cost half as much.

The wardress retrieves the lot with an air that mixes distaste (her nose twitches fastidiously as I hand them to her) and suspicion ("Wasn't there a belt with this?").

Is it any wonder this treatment sends me flying to the specialty shop, where I am promised friendly, personalized service?

I am, in fact, scarcely in such a store before I am accosted by no less a person than madam owner herself, who assures me any doubts I have about the clinging crepe in the window that I am considering will be dispelled the moment I try it on.

The fitting rooms are even smaller than the department store cells and, since madam does not wish the customer to make an evaluation on her own, do not have mirrors.

"Just come out when you have it on and I'll zip you up," the lady suggests.

Once this is accomplished, the pair of us step up to the

mirror to assess the effect — a privilege everyone else in the store is also afforded. I realize I would never have known if I had not tried this dress on how lumpy I am capable of looking.

"You were made for this dress," madam gushes. "It is you!"

If it is, kindly shroud me with a dust sheet, I wish to say, but what comes out is: "It's not quite what I had in mind."

While madam is not prepared to retreat from her stand that the dress captures the essential me, there are, fortunately, several others equal to the challenge. Hastily, she pulls them out, one after another. Politely, I demur, wishing only to shed the garment and, having caught the smirks of other customers, the humiliation that goes with it.

Madam's mood, so sunny a moment before, darkens.

"Thank you for letting me . . . ," I begin, but she has already turned her back.

I slink into the changing room. Even though I can scarcely bend an elbow, I feel I am morally obliged to remove the dress myself. In the tiny space, I throw my neck out reaching for the zipper, which I then manage to embed in my flesh.

"Ow . . . ouch . . . aahh . . . eeee!"

"What's going on in there?" madam demands, her voice suggesting that I am using the occasion for some particularly disgusting cult ritual.

"Nothing . . . I . . . oh . . . ow . . ." The pain is unendurable, but I cannot ask for her help. She has already shown to what lengths she will go to sell this dress and would not, I feel sure, be above deliberately damaging it and then holding me responsible. With a superhuman effort, I suck in my stomach, shrink myself an entire size, catch a fleeting glimpse of how the dress *could* look, and dislodge the zipper.

In returning the dress to her, I try to soften the disappointment by handling it with the same reverence I might show robes of state. "It's so gorgeous. If only I could do it justice," I say humbly.

But she is not deceived and takes the dress with a shrug. Perhaps she glimpses under this craven attitude the girl who once squandered lunch hours with her pals at the millinery bar. The one who laughed so hard at the others, but thought the sight of herself with a cluster of poppies erupting on her head one of the loveliest on earth.

Ah, if only I could recapture that feeling now!

Perhaps I could, if I could send someone else into the fitting room for me. A stand-in. It wouldn't have to be human. It could be one of those rubber dolls lonely guys have found to be such a comfort. Deflated, it would go with me everywhere, to be brought out and blown up (rate of inflation pegged to figure fluctuation) when needed for try-ons.

With such a surrogate, I wouldn't be dashed by disappointments and, if there were triumphs, I'd savor them to the full later.

That's what I want — to bypass trying on and go directly to dressing up. Just as, come to think of it, I did as a girl. Only this time the clothes would fit. And they would be mine.

On the Waterfront

The rest of the year we were typists and telephonists, but on our two-weeks-holiday-with-pay, tottering about on high heels in swimsuits that looked like girdles, we were bathing beauties.

"I could have been a contender," I think of my days on the waterfront in the early 1950s. If I wasn't, it was my own fault. I never, except indirectly, competed in a beauty contest. My feeling that such an event was an affront to human dignity was confirmed when, as a nine-year-old, I entered, in my swimsuit, Uncle Peter's Seaside Amateur Show and sang, "I don't want to set the world on fire."

"No fear of that, kid," Uncle Peter assured me — a devastating assessment, since we were to be judged on cuteness as well as talent. When the audience was asked to appraise my performance, the patter of applause was so weak it might have been nonexistent had it not been for a rare show of support from my brother.

His gesture may have been prompted by the fact that he

had won a contest (Most Beautiful Baby, 1934) and from that pinnacle was prepared to give me a hand up. Mind you, he had been entered — a distinct advantage over entering yourself — whereas I had pretended to be my proud mother when I sent in my picture after deciding to help the *Sunday Pictorial* find Britain's most beautiful girl.

In submitting my likeness rather than myself, I was following in the tradition of those pioneer beauty contestants of the 1850s who, while reluctant to appear in person, had deluged P. T. Barnum with their daguerreotypes in the hope of having them exhibited in his Congress of Beauty Gallery, where visitors could vote on who was choicest. The judging of cakes, babies, flowers, and cows had always brought in the crowds, so why not women? P. T. had reasoned. But even though he offered a diamond tiara if the winner was married and a dowry if she wasn't, he couldn't get the ladies to compete until he said they didn't actually have to appear but could send pictures instead; and he even promised to withhold the names of those winners who felt the exposure might threaten their respectability.

The *Sunday Pictorial* withheld names too. All but the ten finalists. The rest of us were acknowledged with ". . . our thanks to the thousands and thousands of lovely British girls. . . ." For a while I drove myself mad with thoughts that I was number eleven or that the paper had never even *seen* my picture, since, true to their word, they did not send it back.

That was my only formal attempt at bathing-belle recognition. After that I looked for it by loitering with intent to attract a passing talent scout who would waive the embarrassing preliminaries and have me crowned Beauty-Queen-by-the-Sea and photographed for all the papers with two pretty but undistinguished girls flanking me as runners-up.

For me, the beauty bout was never an end in itself. That was for silly little starlets like Joan Collins, Debra Paget, and Terry Moore. No, for me the contest was a career short-cut — once I was honored as a bathing beauty, it would be that much easier to seek acclaim as an author/actress/star, and I need never wear a swimsuit again. At least for professional purposes.

But when I returned to the office from my seaside holiday, it was not to make a splash in the typing pool with my contract from MGM, but with snapshots of Ian of Liverpool, who *had* been captivated by my charms.

These romances lasted no longer than the tan, the fading of which was a greater cause for regret. It was harder to come by, for one thing. While other vacationers sat in their deck chairs bundled up against the chill, I lay stoically on the stony beach, lashed by the cold winds of a British August and turning blue more often than brown.

A tan was almost as good as a beauty title, and you probably couldn't have gotten the latter without the former. Natural ability to tan may not have been as highly prized as 36-24-36, but it was a plus, like a good head of hair or set of teeth.

I smugly compared myself to a light-skinned friend who, though blessed with better proportions than I, felt her chances in the beauty stakes lessened by the way her skin burned, peeled, burned, peeled (even under the feeble British sun), leaving her with not so much a tan as scar tissue.

Lack of a tan would be no hindrance today. In fact, if medical objections lead to aesthetic ones, we'll soon strive to be as pale as the sands we sit on, protecting our ivory skins as fiercely as those earlier belles with their coy ringlets, dimpled thighs, and vast bottoms.

Annette Kellerman, swimming champ, put them out of business in the 1920s when she set the standard for boardwalk beauty at Atlantic City with broad shoulders and slim hips.

The athleticism that Annette stressed had nothing to do with beach glamour, as far as I was concerned. Swimming was just another subject like geometry that you had no use for once you left school. The girls who kept up the breast-stroke — we were taught in the dreary municipal baths — were the sort who greased their bodies, put on goggles, and tackled the Channel. Freaks. Belles like me bathed for beauty and kept our heads above water, all the better to catch the admiring glance and acknowledge it with a flashing smile as we imitated the Esther Williams backstroke.

On the whole, I preferred to display my form on dry land. Not always easy, what with remembering to suck in my stomach (suits might look like girdles, but they didn't always *perform* like them) and walk with quick steps before my three-inch heels could sink in the sand and put me down in the dumps. In the interests of leggier legs, I wore stilettos even to tan, and when they were off, I acted as if they weren't and went around on tiptoe like a Barbie doll.

The problem of legs is approached today from the other end, as we pretend groins are thighs and hip cuts reach to the waist. There are drawbacks: with exposure of hair never meant to see the light of day, waxing doesn't wane until after Labor Day and, without support, the wobbling bottom sabotages the fiction of the long and *firm* thigh.

Designers like Norma Kamali are lowering the leg on these beach bums, and if Ms. Kamali, who already has a reactionary interest in the corselette, extends the trend into her swimwear, we could be back thirty-five years, plunged once again into the Age of Lastex. Padded and cinched, hooked and laced — after so much emphasis on the open, exercised, outdoorsy body, one that is secret, indolent, and indoorsy would be a refreshing change.

I'd welcome it. And, in fact, I feel I've anticipated the trend, at least so far as an air of mystery is concerned: I float down to the sea in shifts (and other cover-ups). But if you think this is the mark of the beached belle, let me tell you it keeps my bathing-beauty aspirations alive, particularly since, I fancy, the speculation is raised: "Is it possible there is a thrill or two in that plain brown wrapper?"

A Question of Timing

The worst New Year's Eve party for Louise was when she found her husband stripped to his shorts having a diaper pinned on him by a recently widowed blond wearing a beard.

"He's going to be the new year and I'm going to be the old," she giggled.

"That's the first time she's laughed in months," everybody said. Under the circumstances, it seemed tasteless to make a scene and deny the widow the fun of an innocent prank, but Louise did anyway.

"Can't you take a joke?" everyone wanted to know. Everyone, that is, except the widow, who left the party with the husband in hot pursuit.

When Louise told me the story, I couldn't believe she hadn't waited until *after* midnight, when any objection to continued merrymaking with the widow would have been bound to meet with more sympathy.

As it was, reproaches were still on *his* lips when he turned up at lunchtime the next day.

Normally, Louise would have handled a situation such as

this with precision and polish; but I shouldn't have been surprised that she botched it on this occasion because almost everyone's timing is off on New Year's Eve. Rare is the person who can strike it right. For most of us, it's a matter of going to the wrong party, giving the wrong party, planning it too early, starting it too late.

Perhaps the major reason is that on New Year's Eve we're never quite sure if we ought to be determining our fate or submitting to it — will something magical just happen or should we arrange for it?

But whatever we do almost always falls short of the occasion we've been conditioned to expect.

Deep in my heart I know that there is only one sort of New Year's Eve party. It takes place on a transatlantic liner. I'm wearing white satin and looking like Carole Lombard. My partner for the night resembles Gary Cooper and dances like Fred Astaire. An Edward Arnold look-alike is my crusty but doting daddy, and he's just slipped another round of diamond bracelets on my arm. Balloons and streamers float overhead. I am wearing an adorable paper hat. We are all drinking champagne.

I will never go to such a party, since the whole thing sank without a trace in 1937.

Nothing has risen to replace it, or if it has, I'm moving in the wrong circles. The commonplace little affairs I have attended over the years fall far short of this exhilarating standard — as New Year's parties do for most of us.

Even if we have an invitation, say, to go to Spain, we will find ourselves in some café in Granada listening to a flamenco singer wailing about her lover's thighs as we sip wine with a man in a plaid jacket who asks us not once but fifty times: "Is this the life or is this the life?"

Desirable men do not have to mount expensive expeditions to get a New Year's date.

On the contrary, myth has it that this elusive breed does not date at all on New Year's Eve, but comes alone to parties with the sole purpose of finding that certain someone interested in commitment to a well-heeled, irresistible human being. Is this any time to be out of the country with a man you wouldn't go to a movie with?

As someone who has always lost more men than I've found on New Year's Eve (beginning with Cliff, when I was fifteen, who kissed Esme at midnight and stayed clamped to her from then on), I expected to have a respite during my domestic days, when New Year's could be looked upon as nothing more than a Christmas repeat — except we took down the tree on New Year's instead of putting it up, and nobody said it was too commercial or that you only celebrated it for the sake of the children.

It was *because* the children were left out that I had an interest in New Year's Eve. Just the same, more than one party was marred by childish antics — the merry-widow story was by no means an isolated one.

New Year's Eve depends on your life at the time. If I ever gave up New Year's completely, it would have to be because every night was so riddled with significance that it wouldn't occur to me to attach any importance to that particular one. Then I could be like an old Air Force friend of my husband's who delivered jets (and other things, I shouldn't wonder) around the world and when asked where he'd be on the night of nights, would say, "Somewhere over the Sahara, I imagine."

I often thought of him coming to one of our New Year's Eve parties and finding them as curious as those festivals intrepid travelers used to stumble across: ". . . we arrived during Mukayuk . . . finding the natives silly on fermented rhubarb juice and decorated with feathers and paint . . ."

I've got to say it was the feathers-and-paint aspect of my own yearly rituals that rarely disappointed me. Half the fun was getting ready (once the evening was over, it might look closer to ninety percent); at that point, I was still hours away from the realization that the toilette so stunning set against home surroundings would pale considerably compared to the finery in a roomful of special effects.

I distinctly remember the year when I had been given a huge box of makeup for Christmas by the publicity woman of a cosmetics house. As I recall, I didn't have a particularly exciting evening dress, but I thought my face would more than make up for it. I applied shimmering violet to the eyelids, painted the lips iridescent brick, and had scarcely finished the last dab when I experienced a wave of turbulence that brought a greenish tinge to the ivory sheen of my skin.

Intestinal flu had struck. It raged unabated throughout the night. But the next day, I was not sorry that it had kept me from going out. Not only could I still nourish the dream of stopping men's hearts with my loveliness, I didn't have to cope with a hangover. On the contrary, I was totally drained, cleaned out, and ready for the year ahead. Sipping tea and munching on dry toast on New Year's Day, I cannot remember feeling more optimistic.

Usually such a disturbance marks the start, not the end of the year, and I have found that when I've gone from party to party, I have been especially vulnerable. First of all, the night air is just enough to disperse whatever measure of euphoria I may have acquired, so I have to redouble my efforts to get into the spirit of things on arrival. And then, even if

I'm wise enough to stick to one type of liquor, the variation in quality from one place to the next can be seriously indisposing.

Party hopping really doesn't have much to recommend it, particularly when each new affair looks remarkably like the one you've just left. Same people, same music, same buffet table — the high altar of these events, desecrated by careless snackers who have littered it with paper plates on which they've mixed cheesecake and chili and left a drift of cigarette ash over the potato salad.

It is usually around five in the morning, when I am yearning for bed and for something to neutralize my digestive system, that I come on the most sickening sight of all: the party where the table is newly laid and the lamb as yet uncarved.

It is then that I am likely to cry. What's food got to do with New Year's Eve anyway? Carole Lombard never ate anything, except maybe a bead or two of caviar.

In the cold, gray dawn of January 1, there is nothing left but resolutions. The usual: keep fit, keep calm, keep up, get thin, get smart, give up New Year's Eve parties.

I know I won't. What I might do, though, is be like the girl who, when asked what she was doing New Year's Eve, said "Nothing."

"Who does she think she's kidding?" the envious asked, convinced she really had something special on that she was unwilling to share.

Perhaps she did. In any event, it's the only way I can see to put New Year's Eve in its place.

So I, too, have been saying "Nothing," with an enigmatic smile, hoping that everyone else, at least, will think my New Year's Eve will be what it was always meant to be — one of unimaginable dazzlement and delight.

Every Breath You Take

It is not what you smoke, but how you smoke, that counts. Who knew what brands the all-time greats — Bogart, Bette, Marlene — smoked? Flashing the pack, especially if it's foreign, can have a certain cachet; but designer cigarettes — like Yves Saint Laurent's Ritz brand — and menthols can never be elegant.

Never a distinguished smoker myself, I have always admired the habit in others and am sorry to see how little brilliant smoking there is today. That air of glamour and sophistication that used to mark the smoker has all but disappeared from those who gamely carry on. But how can you look poised and polished, seductive and slinky, or tough and resolved when you're flying in the face of medical opinion and public disapproval?

It was a different story when I was growing up and cigarettes were a must. There was something missing in people who didn't smoke. Either they were immature, or worse, nature lovers. A cigarette was the finishing touch. As, alas, it so often turned out to be.

But far from regarding smoking as a risky business, we believed it to be beneficial. Serious constipation, nervous disorders, and mental disruption awaited those foolish enough to give it up and there were grave questions about the moral fiber of those who never started in the first place, as Compton Mackenzie pointed out in his 1940s tract *Sublime Tobacco*, which selected Hitler, "that non-smoking lackey in his lavatory attendant's uniform," as a prime example.

Right was on the side of the smokers and to do it well you studied the stars. My ideal was Simone Signoret. She smoked in almost every one of her movies, and since I couldn't do *anything* without a cigarette, I had lots of opportunities to ape her. I couldn't work, play, eat, concentrate, relax, or fall in love without smoking and I swore I could never love a man who didn't simultaneously light my cigarette (as Paul Henreid lit Bette Davis's in *Now, Voyager*) as well as his own.

I found one and married him, expecting that the cigarette would continue to help me express myself as a fully realized human being. But instead I found I could not raise a family, run a house, *and* put away a pack a day with polish.

"I have only one pair of hands," I would cry in despair, dismayed that they had been perfectly adequate for flirting and smoking but were quite unequal to the task of cleaning and smoking.

Unable to smoke and scour the sink, I'd leave the cigarette to burn itself out on whatever was handiest. Once I left it on the edge of the kitchen counter and my husband, who wearily perched there after a careworn day, gave himself a smoldering bottom and an aversion to me that he never really overcame.

I could have given up housework and smoked instead, but was that the image I wanted? Besides, the children were contemptuous enough. When my daughter Rebecca's teacher asked if I had a hobby, Bex replied: "She smokes. But she's not very good at it."

I hated being thought of as an amateur and this, as much as the surgeon general's warning, was why I stopped. I couldn't blame my failure on domesticity. The fact was that I was not a naturally gifted smoker, because gifted smokers don't need ideal conditions. They can smoke in a tropical downpour or while they are doing the tango. Nothing stunts their style.

But then, I don't come from a line of great smokers. My father was an annoying, emphatic smoker who made popping sounds when he puffed. My mother was a secret smoker while he was alive, which was odd, because she openly defied him in everything else. When she smoked in front of others, she still did it as if she might be found out any minute — going at it fast and furiously, flapping the air with her hands. It was a relief to us all when she took up smoking in secret again in her eighties.

These days the world is full of people who smoke the way my mother did — either secretly or with that strained, apologetic air. As a nonsmoker, I find that the smokers who get on my nerves are those who try to be unobtrusive — like the man who holds his cigarette behind his back, giving me the sickening impression that he is charring his palms.

The smoker I like to be around is a friend of mine who smokes with dash and reckless abandon whenever he has just arrived home from writing assignments in Central America. But it doesn't last. He becomes as uncertain and abject as anyone else once he realizes he's back in a world where the imminent danger is the cigarette, not the death squad.

Of course, even in the United States there are places where hopes are low, opportunities limited, and smoking the least of your problems. These are ideal conditions for RJR Nabisco (successor to the R. J. Reynolds Tobacco Company) and Yves Saint Laurent, and if they can find large numbers of the stylistically gullible in these circumstances, more power to them. But puffin' on the Ritz isn't going to make smoking chic again.

If Ritz succeeds, other designers will want to exploit this type of licensing opportunity. Significantly, Bill Blass has already been shown smoking in his perfume ad. How much longer before he, Oscar de la Renta, or Calvin Klein will be rolling their own?

They can be sure of one thing. Whatever they blend, however they package, they won't be joining Saint Laurent in giving the world the equivalent of the *dernier cri*, the last gasp. Because if there *is* any style to smoking left, you can be quite sure the designer cigarette will kill it off.

Abreast of the Times

I suppose we women have all felt betrayed by our bosoms at one time or another.

"Daphne is *so* developed," we English schoolgirls would say, scathingly, of some unfortunate with a noticeable bust-line. It was hard to think of anything more contemptible.

I was in despair when it became apparent I would soon be in Daphne's condition and tried to disguise it by eating myself into a state of overall portliness ("May I have another helping of plum crumble, please?") on the theory that it was better to be fat than developed.

Before the swell of midriff could equal bust, deliverance arrived in the shape of the American sweater girl, personified by Lana Turner. Lana's woolly uplift was a national as well as personal asset. Pinned up on barracks and stenciled on bombers, it led the way to victory in World War II.

Scorn changed to envy at school. Girls were stuffing bras who'd never even owned them. The Daphnes and Fredas came into their own. Almost.

The breast of 1944 had its specifications. Only the Americans, we believed, knew precisely how to truss a bust for uplift *and* forward thrust. Our dowdy British brassieres lacked the requisite engineering, but we made do by tightening our straps until we had deep ridges in our shoulders and we gave ourselves pointier nipples with padding. We didn't know it, of course, but we had the most assertive breasts since the Edwardians.

Our mothers were shocked. Their bosoms, which had developed from the flattened flapper and the curvier but still unobtrusive model of the thirties, didn't do much beyond bulge. British mums couldn't believe we were stacked for style, not sex. They weren't the only ones.

"British boys are not mature enough for bosoms," I remember saying reprovingly to Basil, after he'd lunged at mine. In his seamy, narrow world where foundation garments sent erotic messages and senses could be inflamed by corsets in catalogs, what would he know of bobby-soxers, soda fountains, and stylish uplift?

What would the French know? They too were unsympathetic to the American *jut* as a legitimate fashion statement. And once the war was over and French leadership in fashiondom reasserted itself, Dior took away our aggressive breasts and replaced them with mild-mannered ones that would not interfere with the line of the New Look. The days when the bosom was allowed to dictate the silhouette (except in the movies and girlie books) were over.

The breast that evolved out of these opposing views was the retroussé Barbie breast, cute as an upturned nose and rarely occurring in real life. Many of us went to bed in our cups every night unable to face the pendulous truth and, perhaps, in the hope that our breasts would eventually assume the shape our bras prescribed.

Father knows breast, we thought, and we'd never get Glenn Ford, the split-level house, and the finished basement unless we got a pair like Debbie Reynolds or Sandra Dee.

We have always tended to believe men are to blame for the shape we're in, but the truth is that men always have accepted a far-ranging selection of bosoms and still do. I have known the same man to be equal to full-breasted and flat-chested women. Look at Carl Bernstein — married to Nora Ephron and her well-publicized flat chest and yet enjoying a fling with amply endowed Elizabeth Taylor.

Isn't it we women who yearn for the uniform breast?

Even when we burned bras and cried, "All breasts are equal, regardless of size, shape, or hang," it had a hollow ring. Breasts went slack, but standards didn't. The ideal unfettered breast called for just a hint of sag, coupled with enough weight to provide the right degree of wobble — too much and you were stuck with ponderous sway; too little, a limp swish.

I can remember sprinting for a bus and a chap I knew remarking as I clambered aboard, "Trust you to be one of the first to go without a bra."

Pleased to be thought principled, I didn't tell him I was wearing one at the time.

But the breasts of many of us bra burners were still under some kind of constraint. His confusion was understandable. The contrast between the implacable bosom sternly uplifted by seamed satin and the relaxed breast barely supported by a wisp of tricot was considerable.

I can remember when the bonny bouncing breast first turned up on TV.

"Jiggling, we call it," a network executive explained, advising me to catch the action on Suzanne Somers on *Three's Company*. There were hopes that jiggling would go far — all the way, perhaps, to Barbara Walters, who would add the eager, questing breast to her apparatus for interrogating showbiz celebrities and heads of state.

The movable breast (like the discernible nipple) has never had broad popular appeal.

Today's breezy Christie Brinkley breast is outdoorsy and fit but fairly static. Unhappily, no amount of fresh air and exercise will give it to us if we don't come by it naturally. For most of us, duplication will depend on a bra, or surgical intervention.

Of course, there are those women who stick to their own no matter what. Dolly Parton would never be bullied out of her breasts. Mindful that the royal bosom must be a cushion for the crown jewels, Queen Elizabeth has had the same bust since she was eighteen. So far, Princess Di's vivacious cleavage has not been converted to the imperial monobosom in the same interest.

Mind you, her breasts will have undoubtedly undergone a change if she suckled her boys (a wet nurse seems rather feudal, after all) and she may have even already had some uplifting work done to return her *poitrine* to its former glory. Breasts have been known to snap back of their own accord; others, once converted to udders, never quite assume their old, carefree ways.

Given this situation, plus the fact that breasts are turning up on the fashion pages, we could be faced with a brisk demand for silicone inflation from those who have dieted away any vestige of breast in accordance with strict couturier demands.

Only the wizened breasts of the elderly will be left alone — or will they? The fact that silicone breasts feel like tennis balls may be of little concern to this group; brisk demand could follow on such inducements as, "It's never too late to have the bosom you always wanted."

Natural breasts, as an aspect of style, have always seemed to show up where they aren't wanted. Perhaps the artificial kind will have more luck.

Tough Girls Don't Knit

I dreamed I knit a tinsel coverlet for Hollywood and when Christo saw it, he said: "I had planned to wrap a river (possibly the Danube) in sheet music, but in the light of her achievement, my idea now seems puerile."

I dreamed I won the world's highest culinary award for pasta knitting — fuselli, cappelletti, capelli d'angelo — with the judges citing: ". . . extraordinary texture *and* taste with phenomenal sauce absorption achieved . . ."

American women don't have dreams like this because they don't knit. They think they're too tough to knit — too glamorous, too smart, too liberated, or too busy.

I'm British, so knitting's in my blood, but I wouldn't be having these dreams if it weren't for superstar knitter Kaffe Fassett. Mr. Fassett juggles as many as sixty yarns, some old and rare, in his sweaters (a strand or two of botany from King George V's muffler, perhaps), and for one of his crewneck pullovers, he will charge as much as $2,395. Despite these distinctions, Mr. Fassett's most singular achievement must be that by knitting together past and present he has reminded me of my knitting roots, so the aspirations I once had are returning to crowd my sleeping and waking moments.

Just last night I dreamed my knitting had the world in stitches and I broke all known box office records. "Comic genius!" the critics raved, explaining, "It's not just how she knits, but what she knits that's the all-time sidesplitter. Her cardigan's a classic and makes Chaplin's tramp suit look about as funny as a Savile Row pinstripe."

Mr. Fassett may have reawakened such ideas in me, but it's because I grew up in Britain (where you cast on at birth, cast off at death, and have a lifetime of woollies in between) that I have them in the first place. In Britain, everybody knits. A bishop knits his own vestments, a chemist knits a tightly clinging tube in sparkle bouclé, a barrister knits the place mats for a dinner she's giving. Britain, no doubt about it, is a Nation of Knitters.

Although there have been sporadic outbreaks of knitting in America (particularly in wartime), it has never become a national pastime. Americans are pragmatic about knitting. They take it up with the sole intention of producing a sweater or a scarf. In Britain, women will knit without apparent purpose for years and years. In America, a woman who does decide to knit will get through it as quickly as she can since it is considered neither a chic, smart, nor youthful thing to do — in fact, to be caught with needles and wool in hand is to age twenty years.

Perhaps if I had stayed in England, where I would not have damaged my image by knitting, I might, by now, be doing it at the cosmic level that I have dreamed about since the age of eight.

At that time I knit an egg cozy. Because of some miscalculation, it came out square and was a slipshod fit. My mother declared it a failure. I, on the other hand, realized that if I had produced a snug fit, I would have been expected to outfit the teapot. I also realized that there is nothing like knitting for letting the mind wander — precisely what knitters are warned against. Had I heeded this injunction, I would have succeeded in covering the egg instead of — far more important — questioning the shape of it.

The opportunity for enlightenment through knitting would never arise for any American because of central heating. Soft-boiled eggs eaten from the shell do not grow cold in America and cozies for them have not been knit here since the nineteenth century.

Still, while I never succumbed to the *craft* of knitting, I grew up, as we all did, wanting to be the girl on the knitting pattern in a twin set and kilt, standing in front of a mock Tudor with a scottie on a leash and a Morris Minor at the door. The difference was that, unlike my friends, I never attempted to knit the twin set and thereby devalue it and all it stood for by making it part of my dingy lower-middle-class world.

In fact, I was still wearing my shrunken pullover (with a hole in the elbow) and knitting for the sake of knitting (a nondescript strip of moss stitch) when I had a vision that took me beyond twin sets and mock Tudors forever: "Sign that enchanting ragamuffin," the famous American movie director said, "and her knitting, too."

It was in my rebellious years, though, that I found I could knit and express my outlook on life. I don't suppose I could have found a more apt declaration of my attitude than the sheer anarchy of my deliberately dropped stitches and determinedly disrupted patterns. And had my work been better known, my decision to float a sweater free of its anchoring rib would be remembered even now as the nude-descending-a-staircase of knitting.

Good God, you may be exclaiming at this point, Rei Kawakubo's made a fortune with dropped stitches and sweaters with holes, and Calvin Klein just recently dared to leave the rib off his five-hundred-dollar cashmeres. Why didn't you stick to being a stylist?

The answer is that I have never thought of knitting as a trade. Even if I were to do it just for myself (knitting a rag rug often seems a possibility), who's to say I wouldn't end up with a revelation instead?

Nevertheless, I think I must start knitting again — always doing it while smartly dressed and reading Proust, to overcome its poor image, set an example, and prove there's more to it than making mittens. It's up to me now — although in the past, it's taken a national emergency to show American women it's not the sock but the *act* of knitting that counts. Let's not forget that women have knit socks for soldiers in wartime when machines could have turned out enough for a standing army in the time it took to turn a heel.

But knitting for morale is one thing, knitting to discover its full power is another.

For this reason, I don't think knitting should be lightly undertaken. Except by men, who could work at getting rid of its craft shoppe stigma, as Kaffe Fassett already has. In fact, I urge him to come home — though from California, he lives in London — and knit Americana, perhaps by recreating the 1940s sweater girl, with yarn from an actual Lana Turner pullover.

However, girls who wish to test their aptitude for *serious* knitting should knit an egg cozy.

Materials: Anything but mohair, which could shed on the egg.

Needles: Small, for dense texture.

Instructions: Pick an egg of the size you usually eat (S, M, L, or jumbo) and measure.

Starting at the top, cast on a small number of stitches and knit, increasing at the beginning of each row; or, starting at the bottom, cast on a large number of stitches and knit, decreasing at beginning of each row. Make two pieces and sew up.

Try on egg.

If it doesn't fit and you have the guts to blame the egg, you are tough enough for cosmic knitting.

The Older Woman as the Other Woman

When, some years ago, a married colleague had an affair with his landlady, we were scandalized. It wasn't the idea of the affair (we were *all* having those), but the fact that the woman was older and taller than he.

The whole thing seemed unnatural — particularly when we met her and she turned out to be fifty, fat, and, most incongruous of all, jolly. She was an amateur singer of light opera, liked to bet on the races, and had a dachshund called Ron, but none of this was enough to overcome her anti-romantic image. To do her justice, she was as baffled to find herself in the role of mistress as we were. "God knows what he sees in me," she said, with a chuckle. "I suppose he just needs a bit of cheering up."

We were shocked that anyone could commit something as serious as adultery for nothing more than a few laughs. Of course, it came as no surprise that when the wife got wind of it the outcome was as feeble as the affair itself and the only thing that happened was that the landlady missed a month's rent while looking for new tenants. What else could you expect? we asked, comparing the affair with the liaisons we had had with people of suitable age and height that climaxed, in a manner befitting their seriousness, with attempted suicides, disastrous pregnancies, severe weight losses (or gains), and incurable depressions.

The meaning these relationships brought to our lives more than justified any inconvenience they entailed. And although I still believe that no amount of suffering is too great in search of the one true alliance (and also that height is still important), I am no longer disdainful of those who embark on an affair with no other goal in mind than having a simple escapade, even if it does mean going outside of your age group for it.

And, frankly, how else is it to be done? An English newspaper (*The Mail on Sunday*) says that here in the United States there are 108 *young* men for every 100 women. And since the latter figure does not specify, it must mean women of all ages. In other words, a man shortage exists only if you insist on sticking to your own age group, which means slim pickings indeed if you are the older woman.

It may *still* mean slim pickings if you go outside of it. However, you may now be emboldened to do so, and the next time a young man complains that he can't seem to meet a girl, you will boldly suggest, "Come up and see *me* sometime."

Such a move could expose you to an ugly rebuff. It is less likely to happen if you make your overtures to a married man, even if he gets wind of the fact that you are partially motivated in doing so by the need to find *someone* to admire the decades of moisturizing and conditioning that have left you in peak form at sixty. Affairs have been started on far less.

Perhaps you just haven't had time for romance, having known little else but your career. Perhaps he hasn't had time for romance, having married young and known little else but wife, children, and mortgage. Perhaps only a few years separate — but ah, how much wiser you are in the ways of the world! How intoxicated he is by your greater sophistication!

Or is it a mothering instinct you wish to exploit? For those who long to powder bottoms, there is a plentiful supply of childish men who crave such attention.

I have only mentioned three, but there are many more ways to be the other woman and turn what has always been a thankless role into a highly satisfying one. All you have to do is to foot the bill.

You will not resent the outlay. He dreams of nights at the opera. You provide them. *And* supper afterward. And as he listens to you talk about *Traviata* (he didn't know opera existed before *Moonstruck*) with that combination of adoration and awe you rarely excite in a man of your own age, you will congratulate yourself on money well spent.

Can a relationship of such calculation be romantic? Gazing deep into each other's eyes, secure in the knowledge you are each getting what you want — can it be anything else?

It will have been understood from the start that you both have lives of your own and are after distraction without disruption. He wants to protect hearth and home. So do you. Far from wishing him to divorce his wife, you will not even want him staying overnight. You will never sulk because you will be all alone on Christmas (a classic other-woman grievance) since with children and grandchildren of your own, you will be no freer than he is. And if you don't have family obligations, you will want to use the time to check into the spa or some other program of restoration and rejuvenation. Commitments of any kind will be so slight that the breaking of them will not cause even momentary annoyance.

Even from the wife's point of view, there are benefits. If the older other woman is shouldering the expenses (whether that means a few beers or a weekend by the sea), at least the affair won't be a *financial* drain on the man's family. As someone who has been the wife (I seem to have played just about every role in the eternal triangle), the fact that the affair was causing our cash flow to dwindle to a trickle was a greater cause of heartache than any other aspect of my husband's infidelities.

If he'd only taken up with older and more well-heeled women instead of a succession of impecunious younger ones, I would at least have had the comfort of knowing that not only was the whole sordid business being underwritten but that I had youth on my side. It might have been all I needed to decide I was old enough to acquire a *petit ami* of my own.

I could have practiced a little Brie and sympathy on one of the misunderstood adolescents I knew at the time. And if I fancied that I was expanding his peanut butter world, I'd be no different than those lonely dowagers who dreamed of captivating young lovers not only with their wealth but with their wisdom and experience. Alas, it was usually only the money *those* older women had to pass on (if I'd had an affair with a teenager, I see myself setting standards no woman after me could hope to meet), and more often than not, it was the underage gigolo who not only taught these naive benefactresses a thing or two but extracted a high price for doing so.

Things are likely to be different now. If a yearning for romance induces a woman to budget for a boy, along with a cruise or personal trainer, as an essential expense, not only is she likely to get her money's worth, she may well initiate him into the mysteries of brokerage or whatever other means she used to make her money in the first place.

Even if she's not rich, she can, depending on his deficiencies, teach him how to make osso buco or how to behave with his children. As a woman with a past, she can lay glittering retrospectives before him. "You were there!" he will say with wonder as she fills him in on World War II, the Kennedy years, and the Beatles.

She will stretch his mind, improve his prospects, even preserve his marriage. Not a bad deal. It's more than he'd get from a night out with the boys — which, incidentally, is where he can say he's been.

Damaged Goods

My mother used to say I was betraying the starving children of the world if I didn't clean my plate. Perhaps from that notion the belief has grown that I am expressing solidarity with the ragged of the earth by dressing down, if not out.

When, in an excess of moral zeal, I am both overweight and shabby, I fit the profile of the underprivileged person to a T. Recently, in fact, while trundling my shopping cart to the launderette, I was stopped by a homeless man who asked what church was giving away free meals.

Perhaps he didn't see me as a fellow sufferer so much as a person who wouldn't rebuff him. And while I am glad that my clothes make me approachable, I must confess that in cultivating a scruffy air, I am also driven by inverted snobbery. I could not bear to be thought of as arriviste. And almost everyone who is groomed and glossy and defiantly affluent looks arriviste to me. Pat Buckley, Ivana and Blaine Trump, Nan Kempner — *all* those ladies do. And in addition, they look heartless. They may, in fact, spend every waking moment thinking about ways to help their fellow men and women, but that's not what their clothes say.

Now if I had a dime for every outstretched hand I ignore, I could open my own shelter. Yet my clothes say I care and, moreover, are often unkempt enough to relieve me of the burden of doing anything about it — unlike Nancy Reagan, for example, who was obliged to come out against drugs to overcome her wardrobe.

So even though it gives them an undesirable image — not to say a dangerous one in these troubled times — Pat, the Trumps, and Nan insist on everything in perfect condition and nothing but the best. And it's nothing but the best for me, too. Only in my case, it must be flawed, and acquired via the thrift shop, the bargain rack, and the sample sale.

My method guarantees a more distinctive look than Pat, the Trumps, and Nan manage because, although they claim to be deeply committed to individuality and to live in dread of socialist uniformity, they will meekly check into the same de la Renta suit without changing a button. I could never do that. There isn't a designer in the world who, as far as I am concerned, is not subject to revision.

If Kenzo had known how to cut a coat precisely to please *me*, I wouldn't have had to cut the hood off one of his kimono numbers, and Raquel Welch (whom I interviewed while I was wearing it) wouldn't have had to ask, "Was that a Kenzo once?" in a voice that suggested a masterwork had been mutilated.

"Long ago," I murmured, because the coat was a castoff when I got it and its identity had begun to fade even then. But I would have cut that hood off if it had been brand-new — *especially* if it had been brand-new — driven by my need to give it that personal stamp. And since I have neither the time nor the talent, as it happens, to accomplish these alterations except in a crude way, my clothes often end up looking damaged. Because of this, some people think I am a late-blooming punk. But I would never attack Kenzo (or any designer) with a pair of scissors in a spirit of anger, as I believe punks would.

Slashing and bashing by others disturbs me, since I am never sure what's behind it. But if I decapitate a Kenzo kimono, I know *exactly* why I am doing it: first, to show that the hood might be all right for the rest of his customers, but it is not all right for me; and second, through the careless way in which I lop it off, to give the impression that I am chic but so unintimidated by the demands of orthodox fashion that I can look as sloppy as I like.

Untidiness is something I've cultivated ever since I was a kid, but it takes time to achieve it. As long, no doubt, as it takes Pat, the Trumps, and Nan to assemble their immaculate toilette. In fact, they may spend *less* time on themselves, since basically all their clothes have to say is how much they cost and who made them. Their ensembles don't even say Pat, the Trumps, and Nan are gorgeous, since we have often seen the same clothes looking much better on models in magazines.

Not only has no one seen my outfits before, but they impart a far more complex message than anything Pat, the Trumps, and Nan pay Bill Blass to send over. Anything on my back has to speak of my fashion savvy and carefree attitude; it has to show me as a person who is compassionate and independent and, like the duke in the dirty raincoat, too classy ever to be nouveau.

The duke's raincoat, spattered with mud from his fields, spotted with rain from his sky, says reams about the whole tradition of the British aristocrat. Pat, the Trumps, and Nan may have a history every bit as colorful, but as aficionados of the new, they don't give priority to expressing it.

Like the duke, I do. All of it, happy and sad. Along with the cheerful cockney makeshift element caught in almost everything I wear, the keening of the Irish is recalled in my shapeless woollies, as is the wailing of the Jews in my affection for moldy frock coats.

With requirements like these, you can see why it's difficult for me to pick clothes from the rack. But it won't surprise you to learn that there was only one occasion in my life when I took to wearing a brand-new garment without laying a finger on it first.

I was living in Canada at the time, and I craved a fur coat — not because of the weather, but because fur coats, which had always seemed cumbersome and stuffy, suddenly started looking reckless. Maybe it was the fact that a lot of pop stars were wearing them then. In any event, I wanted to be daring and have one.

I went to a furrier and asked him to make one of his regular muskrat styles bordered with raccoon, full length. He'd do it, he said, but full length wasn't customary and it wouldn't work. It didn't. At calf length, it had a slight flare; extended to the ankles, it widened in embarrassing ostentation. My colleagues at the CBC said it looked like Ivan the Terrible's bathrobe — something he'd wear while wandering the icy halls of the Winter Palace.

The coat became known as Ivan the Terrible and I was named Freda the Contemptible because the sight of us together turned my fellow workers into rabid antifur activists. Not only was I harassed by them, but wherever I went, I was set upon by packs of wildlife preservationists who would shower me with pamphlets and lecture me in an abusive manner. In vain, I would argue that these animals were raised for wearing, like battery chickens were raised for eating, and that, in fact, I should be venerated as the savior of the hard-pressed fur industry because I selflessly ordered a coat with so many pelts in it.

I began to hate Ivan and the untenable position he had put me in. I thought of cutting him down to size so he wouldn't attract so much attention, or of turning him into tippets, cossack hats, and muffs. And then the answer came to me! In buying and wearing him *as is*, I had gone against my deepest fashion instincts. I had to rise up against him. Overthrow him. Degrade him. I used him as a car rug. I left him out in the rain. I let him swelter all summer long in a hot and humid closet. By the next winter, he had aged fifty years. He was mangy and decrepit. He was still called Ivan the Terrible — a reference now to the terrible shape I'd put him in — but nobody bothered to castigate either of us except my husband, who was furious that there were still eighteen easy payments to be made on him.

And worth every penny, I thought. Youthful and lustrous, Ivan had been worthless; as an instant antique, he was of inestimable value because he preserved my fashion integrity. Wrapped in His Shabbiness, I felt as if I had been banished by the Bolsheviks yet still bore traces of imperial splendor. In short, I felt like a million rubles.

I have never again thoughtlessly put on some garment, new or not, without rendering it (if not actually rending it) unfit to wear. By anyone but me.

Attack of the Killer Sunrays

The news that another break in the ozone layer has been reported has been warmly received in cosmetic circles.

"Since industrial growth is impossible without environmental mishaps, we can at least take heart from the spectacular potential they offer to the cosmetic industry. The market is limitless," Dr. Barry du Barry of Elspeth Larder said jubilantly.

"And it isn't just the sun," Dr. du Barry added with enthusiasm. "A woman's complexion is raped by toxics and pollutants every time she puts her face out of the door, every day of the year!"

This situation has resulted in a growing number of "skin prisoners" — women who refuse to leave their homes for fear of being assaulted by the environment. Larder is offering new hope for them with its En Garde! — a glaze that hardens into an enamel-like coating and is applied by a professional visagiste. Until recently, Maureen ("Babycakes") Radish rarely emerged from the plastic, atmospherically controlled tent pitched in her Trump Tower apartment. Now she is out and about, her face protected by En Garde! And although the procedure is costly — each application is about $200 — it can be removed without assistance; once safely in her tent, Babycakes Radish cracks it off with a small, solid-gold hammer custom-designed for her by Paloma Picasso.

The firm is developing other skin defenders by trying them out in some of the harshest locations and most hostile climates on earth. In Botula, New Jersey, Larder gels and creams are tested for their ability to repel harmful chemicals by being buried for months on end in toxic waste.

Dr. du Barry admitted that experiments among the Xhuxhi (pronounced "Cheeky") nomads of the African desert were canceled after it was discovered that the tribespeople had used moisturizer and sun-blocking products to keep their camel saddles supple.

"We are now working with the Khnmhn [pronounced "Konmen"] and initially we had some problems. They were testing skin defenders incorporated into cosmetics — blush, lipstick, eye shadow, foundations, and so on — and wearing them violated certain taboos. Fortunately, we were able to arrange for a special dispensation from the king of the Khnmhn, something of a God himself, in exchange for a date with Iman and a permanent credit line at Giorgio Armani. These extras were in addition to the very generous fee we are paying these people to wear the products daily for the next six months," Dr. du Barry explained.

Controversy surrounding the company's global experiments is not always so easily settled. Larder has been criticized for its use of whale blubber, an endangered commodity, to develop an antiaging mousse. Blubber, which was once part of the daily diet of the Eskimo, has become, because of its present scarcity, a prized delicacy and is known as Eskimo caviar. An attempt by Larder to provide the Eskimo with Bluffer, a product touted as a fluffy blubber substitute recycled from truck tires, has met with poor response: "It tastes like burnt hair," the Eskimo say.

"Frankly, I am sick and tired of these people," Dr. du Barry confessed. "Bluffer is a lot less fattening than blubber, is vitamin fortified, and cost us a fortune to develop. If you asked the public at large what was more important — keeping American skins youthful as against making a few changes in the Eskimo diet — I know what their answer would be."

Such conviction has led to the formation of Save Our Skins (SOS), the national organization cochaired by Nancy Reagan and Joan Collins that works to counteract negative publicity directed at cosmetic development.

Loose Living

"We must never think of our comfort," Quentin Crisp warned in a fashion interview he gave me.

I quite agree.

It's not my comfort I am thinking of when I see the years of living loosely drawing to a close. It's my peace of mind. Because loose means anything goes, and fitted means it doesn't. Broadly speaking, conforming clothes move into the body; nonconforming clothes hang loose — even if you happen to be wearing skintight leather.

I knew it was coming. Early warning signs were spotted at the beginning of the Reagan regime, when dress codes were imposed and White House secretaries were banned from wearing pants.

By the spring of 1986, the Reagancy look, characterized by fitted, waisted fashions, was top of the charts. It lingers still.

It has about it the air of the fifties, that era of witch-hunts and all-in-one girdles that had all the flair of an actuarial table. (If you want to get a fix on it, think of Mamie Eisenhower's hairdo and the fact that it was copied by schoolgirls.)

The fifties era suited Nancy Reagan — revering, as it did, the smart young matron, a role Nancy continues to occupy as she creaks into the twilight years. But in 1957, her type began to decline as Dior, who had insisted on that look ten years earlier, banished the waist and got women into the sack.

As James Laver, the fashion historian, once pointed out, the waist in the wrong place (either very high or very low) is a sign of social upheaval and the abandonment of accepted standards of conduct. With the abandonment of the waist altogether, loose living was bound to follow.

Reactionaries were outraged and thundered that the sack, by ignoring the shape, was an insult to womanhood. Oblivious of the slight, women accepted the transformation from curvy ladies-in-waistlines to hussies-in-sacks and said, "My body is my own business." (Although some added: "If you want to make it yours, I am open to discussion.")

By the time we swung into the sixties, we were roundly abusing the old ways — burning our bras, baring our thighs, shrouding ourselves in ethnic tents from muumuus to djellabas.

The couture was bewildered but it adapted. Saint Laurent went see-through and the duchess of Windsor begged Courreges to tog her out in his little white space smock with matching booties.

"Fashion has taken to the streets," Chanel cried in the midsixties, recalling what she herself had done forty years before, when she'd set the style with glass beads and jerseys pinched from the proletariat.

But when the Reagancy ladies pinched from the proletariat, it was not, of course, style they stole. Socialites no longer cared about copying teenage cockneys.

You wouldn't catch the Reagancy looking for fashion handouts from pop circles either. Betsy Bloomingdale didn't care *what* Cher was doing with her hair. The stodgy flamboyance of Joan Collins got the gracious Reagancy nod for acceptable excess.

"You don't want to make an exhibition of yourself," my mother, who would have fit right in with the Reagancy, used to say to me. Oh, how dearly I did! And in the years of living loosely, I had the license to do so.

As I have grown older, permissiveness has waned, but not before I had a fair fling at being Secondhand Rose, queen of the Gypsies, or anything else I fancied. And like thousands of others, I reported for work in any number of extravagances, including a nun's nightie (true, I was a broadcaster and not a bookkeeper).

Let me tell you about the nun's nightie. In all the years of living loosely, that garment grips me more than any other. It was loose in shape as well as in spirit, reached the floor, had a high, square neckline, tight sleeves and armholes ("We must never think of our comfort!"), and was made of a wonderful cotton in a heavenly shade of palest pink.

I wore it all one summer. I boarded planes in it. Danced in discos in it. Even went to church in it. Sightseeing in Exeter Cathedral, I was mistaken for a member of a sect by an eager young curate who extended to me the professional courtesy of a private tour.

I enjoyed the nightie so much it saddened me that the loosening of dress codes, which permitted me to wear it, probably deprived real nuns of the same opportunity. Now that their habits were reformed, they undoubtedly wore street-length ones both by day and by night.

In a broadcast, I asked a mother superior about this very point. "We dress to reflect the community we serve," she explained, demonstrating that the church is no different from the rest of us: Nancy doing her bit in Reagancy Rich and me in Misfit Chic.

Although I have my quarrels with the pope, I am glad to see *he* clings to his old habits, what with all the traveling he does. Whatever else he may have to put up with, it is certainly not binding at the crotch — a complaint that plagues all men, jet-setters or not, and one that Swedish scientists have said poses more of a problem than the dangers of radiation. Hardy Amies says men are anatomically unsuited to trousers, and he *makes* them. The years never got quite loose enough for men, did they?

I shall go on wearing loose as long as I am thin enough to do it. Particularly now, under the lingering spell of Reagancy, when loose is still approved only for the pregnant and the overweight — which is a shame, because they wear it with an air of apology. Fat people who are firm should take pride in their flesh and fit it.

Of course, they won't. The stingy contours of the Reagancy ladies are still in evidence even though portly Barbara is in the White House. And you *really* cannot be too thin or too rich. Too bad the luxury level is dull and shallow — but then, I suppose that is inevitable when it celebrates affluence rather than opulence.

It's not very exciting, though. I mean, you see Nancy and Betsy and Candy Spelling in their Reagancy finery and you don't think of lives risked in quest of gems to bead the bodice, but of cardiac arrest over the corporate merger; you don't think of acres of sable and sacks of emeralds, but of the awesome extravagance of nuclear warheads. To the Nancys, the Betsys, and the Candys, clothes are an *investment*, and maintenance of them is paramount. Not for them the world of carefree upkeep I once saw practiced by a Turkish heiress, who dropped her diamonds into a champagne flute of Windex to bring up the sparkle.

That's the sort of flair that brings to mind marble palaces, silks to squander, and a brace of wolfhounds dyed to match your hair. Not what you get from the stately Reagancy ladies with their condos and limos, high rises and photo opportunities, tax shelters and lobbyists, art bought for investment, and culture ingested in easy doses (highlights and extracts only, please).

The message Reagancy chic would like to send is "We're so rich because we're smart." But how smart are they? Was Nancy's wardrobe for her role as drug crusader smart? If we're to believe the TV movie-of-the-week on the torments of teens in affluent households, clothes like hers turn kids on to, not away from, drugs.

That's what happens when you attempt to champion the privileged and comfort the afflicted at the same time. Lady Bountiful dressing always has been an awkward business, but the British are good at it. Study the queen, Nancy.

If I were a kid, the sight of Nancy would fill me with mighty dread. But maybe that's because she reminds me of the first office manager I worked for, who ordered, "No ankle strap, three-inch heels, please."

Ankle straps in my dingy world as a London typist were my one link with American-showgirl glamour. Such deprivation was not to be borne, so I quit. This gesture of principle normally would have been foreign to my nature, but I thought the seriousness of the provocation demanded it.

It looks as if I might have to take a stand again. If this sermon has alerted you to the dangers, I hope you will buy nothing for spring that is on the Reagancy chic list.

In other words, if the dress looks as if it would be good at selling real estate or at a Trump Tower cocktail party, pass it up.

Strike a fashion blow for independent thought and a world loose enough for any look you fancy. (Even Nancy's, as long as it's drag.)

The fate of the world is not only on your shoulders.

It's on your back.

A Nice Cup of Tea with My Tea

Can the British be trusted to keep the tradition of afternoon tea alive?

My American friends do their bit to encourage its preservation when they visit England. Pilgrimages are made to Brown's or Claridge's. But even as the scones and sandwiches are savored, there is the nagging thought that the commercial version falls far short of what is offered in the average English home, and I am envied my chance to get it.

The truth is that anything eaten between the hours of four and six is "tea" to my relatives. And since they assume that bread and jam, cake and "a cuppa" will affront the sophisticated New York palates of my daughters and me, they are inclined to offer us spaghetti and milk shakes and Chablis and takeout curry instead.

They themselves stick to strong, sweet tea, the sort Britons have drunk for two hundred years and through two world wars. My own mother, when asked what kept her going through the blitz, lightly dismissed the leadership of

Churchill and the example of the royal family: "We couldn't have done it without tea," she said.

In World War I, it was tea*time* the poet Rupert Brooke missed when he wistfully inquired from the Dardanelles:

> *Stands the clock at ten to three*
> *And is there honey still for tea?*

Only in certain circles, Rupert, the answer would be today. A growing number of hotels and restaurants, if not refusing to serve tea, resent having to do so. As for tea shops, when Robert Morley, actor/writer and dedicated teatime man, looked in the London Yellow Pages for one, he found but a single entry: Capone, A, Churlington Street. On phoning, he was told this was a tearoom for workingmen and should Mr. Morley turn up expecting gentility and seedcake, he was doomed to disappointment. Well, the laboring classes have to have their tea, too — although it wasn't originally intended for them.

The Duchess of Bedford, who introduced teatime in 1840, never expected the whole country to turn to it; it was simply a way of keeping the upper crust going between breakfast and dinner. In those days, breakfast was porridge, ham, bacon, sausages, kidneys, boiled or fried or scrambled eggs, kippers, haddock, toast, and rolls. Not surprisingly, it precluded lunch. An afternoon tea of sandwiches, cakes, and buns, arriving at four, must have seemed a gossamer snack amid the Victorian gluttony, and certainly no threat to the appetite that would be brought to the twenty-course dinner ahead.

The excesses of corporate America are of a different sort; but it, too, is taking up afternoon tea to remedy that sinking feeling. Only, in this instance, an executive who's gulped a takeover for breakfast and grabbed a merger for lunch faces his first square meal of the day. Even the business person sufficiently nourished to withstand the Bloody Mary and salted peanut will find the cup of Earl Grey and the cucumber sandwich a better pick-me-up. No wonder afternoon tea is being taken up in the corporate world. Executives rise from the tea table, their wits sharper than when they sat down, ready to carry on through the night if need be, wheeling and dealing and stealing a march on the Japanese — who, of course, have been drinking tea all along.

Mind you, the tea they drink is green (as English tea is, really; it turns black when fermented); and it's good with sushi, if not with scones. But perhaps it's not quite comforting enough to the stressed-out Japanese, who, it is said, are far more likely to turn to whiskey at the happy hour. Maybe the reason the British brew is so black and strong is that it replaced beer as the national drink in England. So miraculous was the nation's emergence from centuries of befuddlement, the British have gone around ever since reminding each other that tea "is the cup that cheers but does not inebriate."

And isn't sobriety precisely what is needed for the happy hour — not only for those bent on business, but for those looking for love and, given the uneasiness of the times, the mild sexual outing? Won't tea for two, exciting the sentimental urge instead of the lustful impulse, hit the spot? And how restful teatime would be for the harried cocktail hostess collapsing under the canapés (no sooner adept at the Spanish tapas than there is a demand for Russian zakuski); she could retreat behind the silver tea service and show that off instead.

Actually, no woman retreats behind her tea set; she is as

much on display as it is. She presides over it, pouring tea and customizing each cup with lemon, milk, sugar, or other flourishes. If she is a dieter, she can fuss with the strainer and tongs, and thus be too busy to help herself to the sweet and starchy treats. Or she may find the ritual improving in other ways — and, like Proust, discover there's nothing like a spoonful of tea and a few cookie crumbs to unleash the mind.

Oscar Wilde demanded rather more sustenance than Proust at tea but nevertheless disapproved of excess. He once rebuked a waitress: "I asked for a cucumber sandwich, not a loaf with a field in the middle of it." A sandwich small enough to be slipped onto a saucer would have been essential for Oscar if the witticism needed a gesture. In fact, this stance was recorded in porcelain when Oscar was turned out as a teapot at the start of the century with a sunflower on his chest and his dangling wrist forming the spout.

Delicacy isn't always stressed. "Nothing is quite so consoling as five sorts of sandwiches and chocolate cake," a portly lady remarked to me as she tucked into a tea honoring Queen Elizabeth's birthday at the Waldorf Astoria in Manhattan. Like many hotels across America, the Waldorf has taken to setting tea tables each afternoon. At the Waldorf, you can also order a cappuccino — which caused one Englishman attending the queen's fete to exclaim: "Coffee at tea! I say, that's going rather far, isn't it?"

I'd noticed him earlier waving away cream with a look of deep disdain, obviously feeling, as George Orwell did, that it gives tea a sickly taste. Orwell, in his essay "A Nice Cup of Tea," set forth eleven rules specifying how the drink should be prepared and served, including the sort of cup to be used (cylindrical), the sort of pot (china or earthenware), when the milk should go in (after the tea), and when tea bags should be used (never).

Orwell, although he championed the lower echelons and even lived among them (*Down and Out in Paris and London*), was born into the upper class, which gave him the confidence to speak out on such matters. I was born into the under class and still feel self-conscious about denouncing tea bags, the adding of sugar, or the serving of muffins in May.

In our house, the milk went in first, the person nearest the pot poured, we shoveled in our own sugar, spread our own bloater paste, and grumbled at the staleness of the cake, baked on Sunday to last all week.

I wanted none of it, and as I toasted my crumpet and chilblains over the fire, I used to dream instead of being a glamorous American girl, sipping an afternoon cocktail, with my long, silk legs wrapped around a bar stool.

I tried to knit her life into mine by going to tea dances, and while other couples stalked around to the quickstep, I'd jive, hissing, "*Swing* it, Nigel!" to my partner and drinking pink gins.

Once I reached these shores, I broke with afternoon tea. But now I am keen to take it up again, particularly since this time around I expect to be better at it: this *is* America, after all, and there will undoubtedly be no lack of experts to tell me how.

In fact, I see myself no longer trapped in the kipper class, serving tea on the lawn, with the sun dancing off my silver and the conversation as light and witty as my sandwiches and cakes.

In the midst of this, a guest overcome by the elegance of it all will be moved to gush: "Only an English person could do it so beautifully."

"Not at all," I shall say. "Afternoon tea is something I picked up in America."

The Stylish Splice

I was recently at my niece's wedding, which was different from any other wedding I have ever attended in that everyone in the wedding party had his or her say during the ceremony.

Naturally, not a word was spoken that hadn't been carefully thought out beforehand. The Bible was revised to remove anything racist, sexist, or extremist (I have never heard God sound so reasonable), and readings from the good book and other inspirational sources were delivered by bridesmaids and ushers. Heartfelt testimonials of their own devising were heard from the bride and groom, who enthusiastically endorsed their parents and then each other. General blessings, both secular and sacred, were bestowed by a justice of the peace and a girl friend studying for the ministry.

I naturally compared this wedding to my own limp nuptials and came to the conclusion that my two sullen affairs weren't so much marred at the altar by lack of chat as by lack of commitment. I blame the substandardness of both my weddings on the fact that I wasn't sure I should be going ahead with them in the first place.

Still, there was at least one similarity between my niece's ceremony and mine. The crying. Acting on the spur-of-the-moment advice of her husband, the mother of the bride was able to stifle the sudden impulse to weep loudly by concentrating on the hat of one of the guests. At my first wedding, I'd asked my brother to ward off Mother's upstaging sobs. I thought he did an excellent job, because when I did catch a glimpse of her, she was not only totally dry-eyed but was standing there with an expression that mirrored my own uneasiness. I later learned my brother had achieved it by whispering, "Did you turn the gas off?"

If all eyes were on me at that wedding and at my second one, they didn't have much to look at (let alone listen to). And I'm sorry now that as a bride I had my greatest opportunity to be in the limelight and I bungled it. That's why, although I wouldn't care to *be* married, I'd like to get married again.

If I did, I'd have a ceremony like the food that usually follows it, which to meet all ethnic and taste preferences often comprises potato salad and tacos, quiche and egg rolls, and pastrami and crab delight all on the same plate.

I'd like such a merry mix for the ceremony. Heavily veiled, I would be borne up the aisle in a swaying sedan chair to the accompaniment of Gregorian chants. The all-faiths ceremony that followed would include inexplicable acts (pulling on the groom's earlobes, perhaps) done for deeply symbolic purposes and the whole shebang would be conducted in a barrage of languages, the most comprehensible of which would be Rumanian.

Apart from the sheer spectacle of the thing, my aim would be to preserve the mystery of the occasion. For I now realize what spoiled my two weddings: I knew what was going on.

The Lost Cause Célèbre

When Lady Mendl (née Elsie de Wolfe), the mother of modern interior decoration, saw the Acropolis, she said, "Oh, beige . . . my color!"

Remarks such as this, which not only maintain the person's celebrity but establish them as endearing personalities, are rarely heard anymore, and it's a pity. I'm not one to deplore the decline in the quality of life (brought up with yellow London fogs, I even think the air is improved), but I do consider it a shame that we no longer get our money's worth out of celebrities.

Perhaps they are not to blame. Perhaps they are no better or worse than they ever were, but have been stripped of their glamour and fascination by the vast and voracious industry that has grown up in this, the first century of assembly line gossip. Certainly, overexposure is feared like a nuclear outbreak. Michael Jackson kept out of sight for a year to avoid it, and Joan Collins might be tempted to do the same if the grim march of time didn't deny her the option.

Those who gamely stay in the public eye may lead lives as wicked and frivolous as celebrities ever did, yet nowadays they feel called upon to strike a virtuous note. As full of self-help tips as Leo Buscaglia, they appear on the talk shows to hype their as-told-to books, stressing that their life stories not only offer such attractions as abusive husbands, drunken, incestuous fathers, and escape to drugs, but the added bonus of rehabilitation through Christ.

Too bad these evangelists are encouraged, particularly in these dark days when the madcap doings of heiresses and stars were never more sorely needed. But instead, we are given the sermon of another remorseful batch checking into Rancho Mirago to dry out. Entering blowsy and fat, they emerge glossy and thin (having shed the empty calories vodka brings), glowing and purposeful, already booked to guest on a soap.

For light relief from these glum doings, I recommend turning to the letters of Colette, where you will find a description of a dinner she had with Lady Mendl (there she is again!), who, at ninety-one, is characterized as "thin, dressed as a schoolgirl and subsisting entirely on alcohol." A marvelous story and the one I prefer to the other, which has Lady Mendl dead by her mid-eighties, having been an exercise fanatic and vegetarian to the last.

I wish Colette were around to issue bulletins about dynamic oldsters of our day whose comings and goings could lighten our gray lives. No one even comes to mind since John Huston died. Instead, we hear about George Burns, who is turned out for the final chapters as a womanizer. It is a useful myth, I suppose, supplying as it does comic material and the decorative touch of an ever-present brace of girls. And given the temper of the times, it offers a chance for

George, one day, to confess to the dangers of late-blooming lechery and to urge others, similarly afflicted, to seek help.

I can hear George now, declaring: "To call such victims dirty old men is the same as calling alcoholics drunks." Thousands will, of course, come forward clamoring to be classified as sufferers. The networks, satisfied that the interest justifies it, will commission a movie and George will star as himself.

A similar outcome could await Sean unrePenntant — renowned for flamboyantly knocking back doubles and bashing photographers — unless he sticks to his liquor and resists reform. But will we find him weakening and, six months from now, chastened, storming the country to push sobriety? And will Madonna, reconciled for this higher purpose, enter into the anti-spirits spirit of things and stand devotedly at his side, renouncing the cross and other blasphemous fashion notes?

In the days when good-time Charlies wouldn't dream of mending their ways, we used to find comfort in knowing that if we weren't invited to cruise on Errol Flynn's yacht, at least our livers were in better shape than those who were. Now *simple* indulgence (never mind overindulgence) is passé. Keeping in shape — almost a corruption of the flesh, when you think of how Sylvester Stallone goes about it — is what obsesses celebrities. Now they not only have the furs, jewels, and mansions, but a circulatory system as unblemished as that of a mountain shepherd, who earns it with a blameless and boring existence of yogurt, grass, and fresh air.

I wouldn't feel so resentful of these advantages if they were at least amusing. When *Vanity Fair* first reappeared, I thought it might be a source for polished gossip. But more often than not, we are expected to thrill to the doings of real-estate brokers — and it is not what the robber baron does on his days off, but his behavior on the job that is scrutinized and passed on to us. Well, I draw the line at financial scandal. I can never understand it, for one thing.

Anyway, sin alone won't do. I want from celebrities what Diaghilev demanded from Cocteau. "Astonish me!" he said; and, of course, Cocteau was nothing if not conscientious in obliging. Cocteau knew that startling news didn't have to be Stravinsky sleeping with Chanel, but could be any revelation of a habit, fixation, or opinion that would cause us to reflect on the famous person, if not on human nature in general. I, for one, would welcome interprofessional bitchiness on the level of that provided by Louise Brooks, who said Garbo made a pass at her and who called Clara Bow a half-wit. Now isn't that an improvement on the sickening spectacle of stars stickily venerating each other as salute follows salute — promiscuously passing out labels like "distinguished," "humanitarian," and "legendary," lest posterity neglect to apply them?

Ultimately, of course, it is the duty of the professional gossipists to let us in on the good and bad; and given what they have to work with, they don't have an easy time of it. Suzy, in the *New York Post*, anticipates the predictability of her subjects with the recurring line "But you knew that" as she provides lists of socialites who trudge from thousand-dollar-a-plate dinner to thousand-dollar-a-plate dinner, led by a sunbaked Douglas Fairbanks, Jr. We can only guess at the squabbles that precede these events as the ladies vie for causes: "It's so unfair, Betsy's got cancer and I'm stuck with Alzheimer's."

Liz Smith, who guarantees celebrities a fair airing,

frequently has a quote of an uplifting nature at the head of her column that sets the tone for what is to follow. Escapades (such as they are) are described with the indulgent air of a good-natured sports teacher. Any wonder that Liz is so beloved by her subjects that when they gave her a roast, the air was thick with tributes? It's not that I want her to imitate the unsavory antics of a Winchell or a Louella and ruin careers or lay lives waste (although it was disappointing to see Imelda so ignored). But the lives of stars as chronicled in today's gossip columns seem no more entertaining than the columns of the accountants who are said to run the lives of those stars.

Better, though, that the lives of celebrities should be heard and not seen. How much more satisfactory to have Cocteau tell us of how the vicomtesse Marie-Laure de Noailles would — lying on the "deathbed" she occupied for twenty years — drop her Turkish rosaries, lick her lips, and keep a salonful spellbound with her ceaseless chat, than to have the whole myth demolished as she is wheeled onto the Letterman show for one appearance too many.

No, unless you are Garbo, you're better off dead if you want to keep the legend alive. Poring over the picture book *The Lives of Lee Miller* by her son, Anthony Penrose, I'm captivated by the history of this remarkable American beauty, who was snatched from the wheels of an oncoming car by Condé Nast and put on the cover of *Vogue* (would he have saved a plain girl?); who lived among the surrealists (especially Man Ray); whose lover crashed his plane to his death after bombarding the deck of her Europe-bound liner with roses; and who, as a war correspondent, was the first to reach Berchtesgaden and freshen up in Hitler's bathtub. But if Lee were here today, would we find her showing up on

20/20 to have the dazzling details of her life reduced to something the average viewer could relate to under the maudlin interrogation of Barbara Walters? If resurrected, would even the wittiest Round Table regulars find themselves running out of wisecracks as they came to us live from the Algonquin every week, with the rhythm of their crackling sallies broken for commercials, news, and weather updates?

Not all is prosaic. Now and then, there's a smidgen of celebrity news that looks promising. I've been following the course of Ira von Furstenberg's romance with Prince Rainier. Ira arranged for the annulment of her first marriage *before* it took place (she seems to have been Drew Barrymore's age at the time) and had her face lifted at twenty-four. She sounds like a gas after the stately Grace. But there are dark rumblings from Princess Caroline, who thinks the romance beneath daddy's dignity and is determined to stop it. Too bad. Monaco would make sense if there were some madness *chez Grimaldi enfin*. What is needed are a few shock waves to shatter the bourgeois calm.

It's a shame Truman Capote isn't around to do it. He was a gossipist without peer and was admired as much for his malice as for the impression he gave that what he revealed to us was the same stuff he dropped into Joanna Carson's ear. Truman said all literature was gossip and, in his case, all gossip, literature. How lovely to read about the lives of the celebrated with never a word about diets and exercise systems, inventories or movie deals! The person who undertakes to write such biographies might balk, wearied at the necessity of being out and about collecting material — in which case it would be perfectly all right to stay in and make it up.

At least that would be all right with me. But then, I'm someone who left school at fifteen, hasn't been back since, and owes much of what I know to gossip. How sad that celebrities no longer set the sort of example that was such an enrichment to me. Sadder still to think there is a Lady Mendl somewhere, but because gossip has become so degraded, she isn't considered worth talking about.

Chairway to the Stars

I have known people mad for bentwood, rocking, swivel, wing, Shaker, reclining, and rush bottom chairs, but my favorite is the Hollywood director's chair.

That chair says Hollywood to me as much as Bogart's trench coat or Betty Grable's legs. It has been on the set from the earliest days of the silent movies, when directors leaning forward in it (and with no soundstage microphone to pick up their words) talked their actors through their scenes: "Now, nibble on her ear. Now, you, my dear, throw back your head and laugh. Yes, yes! Now, kiss her throat."

I'd never seen Bette Davis smoking off the screen until I saw her doing it in her Victorian-governess dress, as she sat in that chair on the set of *All This and Heaven Too*. Up until then, I thought she smoked for the screen only. But here she was, smoking between takes! I felt I was sharing her off- as well as her onscreen moments — moments that would one day be mine when that chair held my starry weight as I waited for the camera's call.

Alas, it was not to be. When the director's chair started appearing in the stores, I thought: Dare I compensate myself for dashed dreams by putting it to service around my dining-room table, or will I be degrading the one thing I have revered for so long?

I decided I would not. After all, why deny myself a chair that was wonderful in its own right, apart from its associations? A chair, moreover, far ahead of its nearest rival, that minihammock, the deck chair. The deck chair has some literary links — the Bloomsbury group taking tea on Virginia's lawn, for example — but is far more likely to recall the vulgarities of the British seaside and, additionally, is difficult to get out of, and not at all adaptable for indoor use.

The director's chair was as practical as it was glamorous. As tough as they come, hadn't it collapsed only in order that it might be carried from studio set to location in the jungles of Sumatra? Wasn't it, after all, from this chair that D. W. Griffith delivered *The Birth of a Nation*? And that Cecil B. deMille, dressed in riding britches and boots and brandishing a revolver, commanded the Red Sea in part in *The King of Kings*? Any chair that could take that certainly ought to be able to withstand the use I intended to give it, as well as any punishment my children might mete out. But it soon became clear that from the director's chairs I owned, deMille couldn't even shout, "Let there be light!" without the vibrations of his voice splitting the seat.

Things went wrong from the outset. I had ordered chairs with black frames and black canvas seats and backs, but the store delivered blond frames with green, orange, blue, and yellow canvas fittings. I should have sent them back, but a dinner party was planned for that night and I thought for once in my life I could have a dinner-with-a-theme — it's fiesta time! — and match paper napkins to chairs; besides, I could always return them the next day. Too late, I discovered that to act on a decorating whim, you need to be rich, or rich enough, when you find your chairs wine- and food-stained the day after, to resign yourself to the fact that no store is going to take them back and to banish them to the greenhouse.

I had no greenhouse to banish them to. Anyway, they were needed in the dining room, so I was stuck with them. I never managed to clean them properly, and they grew ever more derelict as frames became unhinged and seams split. No mystery, I can tell you, ever baffled me more than the fact that a ninety-pound child, passively watching TV, could put greater strain on a director's chair than the bulk of a Hitchcock actively directing a masterpiece from it.

But then no director's chair in studio use ever showed signs of stress. I am quite sure of that. Undoubtedly, it was made by the great carpenters of Hollywood, who would bring to it the same brilliant craftsmanship they expended on the re-creation of Versailles. A lot depended on the director's chair. Still does. A chair even seeming to *sag* under a star would be a disaster of unthinkable proportions. And, of course, nothing — not poor box office, not the contempt of the critics — could undermine a director more than his chair giving way beneath him. Many indignities have been visited on the luminaries of Hollywood, but this particular calamity has never been among them.

When our home was breaking up, we sat down in the director's chairs for a solemn family council. "Your mother and I . . . ," my ex had barely begun, when, with a sound like the passing of wind, the canvas ripped beneath him and he found himself seated directly on the frame. He had expected to direct a high-toned family drama, but found himself the leading player in a two-bit farce.

Afterward, he was bitter that the chair — which had such significance for me — should have played a key role in rendering him ridiculous at a highly serious moment, and he accused me of tampering with it beforehand.

I hadn't. In fact, I was as fed up with those chairs as he was. When I moved to New York after my divorce, I threw them out — saddened that they hadn't seen fit to serve me as well as they had the stars.

When my friend Avril visited me, she was surprised at their absence, since she felt they reflected the true me. It was absurd to think they'd let me down, she said — it was my inexperience in buying furniture (I'd never ventured beyond secondhand shops) that had caused me to make price the first consideration and buy the cheapest version of them I could get. If I got the sturdy, high-quality sort, they would be a handsome reflection of my taste, and I would get the use and pleasure from them that I had anticipated with the first batch.

Well, I thought about it. Top quality would be within my means if I bought just one and, instead of using it for eating, sat in it to work instead. Under the circumstances, I might even have my name printed across the back. And, in this way, I would blend reality and dreams. But having one chair that was mine and mine alone smacked of Archie Bunker and his chair. I might become like him, unpleasantly proprietary, and grow abusive if anyone else dared sit in it.

No, director's chairs belong in my dreams, and they are going to be left there. I won't be tempted to make them part of my life again, despite the fact that I'm always running into them — as I did the other evening, when I discovered a friend of mine had installed them around his elegant dining-room table.

"What made you buy these chairs?" I asked him.

He colored slightly: "I suppose it sounds silly, but they have always had a special meaning for me. I think of myself, sitting on one, outside a bell tent, maps spread before me as I plan campaigns and maneuvers, my turbaned batman hovering with a drink. Or I'm a big-game hunter on safari with a beautiful heiress who has the hots for me. Sitting in these chairs, we discuss the day's kill and plan the night's entertainment, as tom-toms beat in the background, a red sun sinks behind Kilimanjaro, and a bearer brings gins. To me, it's an incredibly romantic chair and yet a highly practical one. It's going to bring an indefinable something to the dining experience here."

He'll learn.

That Old Black Magic

"Why do you say 'fuck'?" I asked a girl of ten when I interviewed a bunch of kids about swearing.

"I like the sound of it," she replied, thoughtfully. "I also like the sound of 'Zsa Zsa Gabor.'" Saying those words together gave the child a frisson of delight, and rather than stunt this response, her parents permitted her to utter them as often as she liked. "Fuck Zsa Zsa Gabor," she would say, not in a dismissive or insulting way, but with an air of dreamy pleasure.

When I was a child, I liked the sound of glamour but was prevented from being as generous as I would have liked in its use. "No, you may not speak of Byron and glamour in the same breath," my English teacher forbade. "It is not only inappropriate, it is insolent and deplorably Hollywood."

Perhaps it was, but I felt about Byron as I did about my Jewish aunties, who, in the midst of World War II — with their shiny silk stockings, their upswept hairdos, their commitment to lipstick, rouge, and mauve eye shadow —

seemed both frivolous and life-affirming in those serious, death-dealing days. They had a mystical, magical quality, just like Byron and Rita Hayworth (who was called the Goddess of Glamour), which would evoke in me a feeling like no other. It is this feeling that causes me to label a baby wearing pearls, or Mother Teresa — whose resemblance to a figure in medieval fresco gives her a glamour that the pope, for all his Byzantine outfits, never has — as glamorous. I have never shrunk from declaring that this one has it and that one doesn't, always hoping my assessments will reach the ears of those concerned.

"I cannot believe she did this to me," I imagine Aaron Spelling raging, because despite his estates, yachts, fleets of cars, and enough gems to feed Ethiopia into the next century, I have cast him among the have-nots.

And although it would be easy enough for him to have himself designated and widely accepted as glamorous elsewhere (given the public's docility in these matters), it is certification by the independent source these people crave — which is why you will find Sylvester Stallone throwing his polo mallet across the room and demanding: "What do I have to *do*, Freda?"

I will tell him there is nothing he *can* do — it's too late now to say *never* ape the upper crust if you want to be thought glamorous; make them copy *you*. That's what Chanel did when she put duchesses into working-girl sweaters and had the duke of Marlborough fawning at her feet. This is why she'd be in the Glamour Hall of Fame if there was one — but there isn't, because such a place would not be glamorous.

Still, if it existed, I'd put Michael Jackson and Marlene Dietrich in it. I think of them as alike for their single-minded pursuit of glamour, as if they were on a quest for the holy grail — which, in a sense, they are; not unlike Diana Vreeland, who with the resounding cry, "Fake it! Fake it!" instructed her minions at *Vogue* to put Cyd Charisse's legs on other models' bodies and achieve "farfetched perfection."

It was only natural that Michael should set himself a similar goal. He has spent his life seeing himself reduced to the simple outlines of comic-book drawings, exploded in a shower of stars in the cartoon animation, rendered larger than life size on posters. It was inevitable that he would find his physiognomy a little mundane; and once in a position to glamorize it, he lost no opportunity to do so. I believe he has done a tip-top job. I don't know why *he* isn't on the cover of *Vogue* as an example of what a make-over can really mean. In my view, he has produced a more glamorous look than Diana Ross, whose image (tacked up beside the cosmetic surgeon?) is said to have guided him on the venture.

When Marlene set about transforming herself a half a century ago, they didn't know then what they do now. Nevertheless, the results were dazzling, with the star shedding the chubby thighs and brunette curls of the Berlin sex bombette to become the world's most streamlined blond. Her sex appeal, like Michael's, was not run-of-the-mill. Marlene then, Michael now, are closer in spirit to those boys who play leading ladies in the Kabuki theater and have a fanatic following as heartthrobs and pop idols among Japanese teenagers.

And who gave more glamour to top hat and tails than Marlene? Well, Fred Astaire, perhaps; but they *were* his working clothes as he went about being the greatest dancer in the universe. Am I risking severe bodily harm from his worshipers if I say Fred never struck me as glamorous to look at? To me, he was godlike when dancing and goofy when acting, but for glamour, he had to be heard and not seen. It is when I listen to recordings of him *singing* that he shimmers with glamour from his top hat to his tap shoes.

For glamour on the dance floor, I'll take a man who has earned the title elsewhere — Humphrey Bogart, John Huston, Graham Greene.

Only Graham Greene is still alive, and it is possible that he would find being singled out by me as embarrassing as getting a humanitarian award from General Pinochet, particularly since I have this habit of using the author's name to describe certain types of glamour: "*Very* Graham Greeneish," I am fond of saying. I once said so to my ex-husband as we watched two men — sunburned, wearing crumpled linen suits, and smoking cheroots — dash onto our plane just before it took off from Miami to New York. My ex, in his summer-weight gabardine, sucking on a Lifesaver to unblock his ears, dismissed them as corporate vice-presidents who had probably gone native while setting up a computer system in the Tegucigalpa branch. If they'd been in Honolulu, he said, we would now find them decked out in leis and shirts printed with tropical flowers and hula girls in grass skirts. He always had a strong reaction when I equated glamour with dishevelment, afraid I would use my outlook as an excuse to neglect his wardrobe and deprive his gabardine of the laundering it deserved.

But glamour doesn't reside in the crease of your pants — Cary Grant's excessive interest in grooming was inclined to reduce the magic — and a persistence in believing it does will keep you from achieving it. It is men like Robert DeNiro, who treat even the greatest examples of the tailor's art with casual disregard, who are glamorous. You can see by Bob's face that he wears Armani, my daughter Sophie says. Precisely.

Audrey Hepburn, I believe, went from bewitching nymphet to faultless fashion plate with only the occasional brush with glamour en route. What has stood in her way? Probably her conviction that being glamorous would interfere with being well-bred, a quality she guards as carefully as her diction.

Cher, like Audrey, is also apt to treat herself like a living national treasure. Cher is descended from Erté (the man whose paintings stud American powder rooms), the Ziegfeld Girl, and the circus bareback rider. And while sawdust and sequins *are* glamorous, it isn't glamorous to suggest that the tinsel tunic is really a hair shirt (oh, those gruesome workouts at the health club), as Cher confides to us the murderous price paid to look like queen of the Nile.

But even if Cher made it seem as if her spangles grew out of her skin (hey, no sweat), getting her own perfume was a move in the wrong direction. Similar action had already destroyed the frail claims Linda Evans, Joan Collins, and Elizabeth Taylor had as glamour girls, and even demolished the stronghold of Catherine Deneuve. It hasn't been glamorous to have your own perfume since Chanel introduced Number Five.

Still, millions will plunk down big bucks on the off chance of getting a whiff of Cher about them. Which may be the reason why Barbra Streisand doesn't come out with a fragrance. Far from encouraging such imitation among the masses, I'd bet she'd see it as the greatest impertinence. I hesitate to pronounce Barbra glamorous in case she sues me ("Who *is* this woman? Call my lawyers"), but I'll take a chance and say that her individuality, often raised to dizzy heights of unique eccentricity, is my idea of glamour.

And there aren't a lot of people (I exempt myself) who would *want* to copy it. For that kind of leadership, look to Madonna, the supreme concocter of melodramas, soon to be seen at your neighborhood mall. Madonna, the ne plus ultra of ringleaders, ends up acting alone because everyone else loses their nerve. So she goes ahead and the rest of the world follows once she's made it safe. Constantly on the move, she is on and off my list, no sooner landing on it with one image than she is off it with another, having lost her place because the latest look doesn't have the qualifying shimmer.

If Madonna is dropped from the roster, it is because she won't stand still. Fidel Castro is knocked off for being too static. If he'd died in office (particularly if he'd been assassinated), he'd be on my list to this day. But he made the mistake of sticking around, cultivating that ridiculous, moth-eaten beard, growing bureaucratic and decrepit, and causing me to wonder why I ever found him glamorous in the first place.

I can't even remember finding another politician glamorous except for Giscard d'Estaing, and that was for his name only. Anyway, he didn't last long.

I am not one of those to make silly pronouncements about the glamour of power (particularly since I believe the combination to be well nigh impossible), nor about the glamour of wealth. Certainly, there's no lack of millionaires eager to prove they are glamorous as well as rich. Take the peppy geriatric Malcolm Forbes, who offers his hot-air balloons and motorbikes as evidence of his worthiness to be labeled glamour boy. But the Disney World stigma surround-

ing his activities deprives him of the title that the late How-
ard Hughes came by naturally. Flying planes, running movie
studios and airlines, designing Jane Russell's breasts, claiming droit du seigneur to astonished stars (he rarely seems to
have missed an opportunity to behave abominably), Hughes
preserved his glamour to the last, reclusively decaying in his
hotel room while ordering people to taste his food in the
despotic manner of some mad, paranoid emperor.

It is said that Garbo hangs on to the century's most in-
violable image of glamour only by staying out of sight.
Those who have caught a glimpse of her report a rather drab
spectacle. This does not detract from her glamour (except for
those who find Joan Collins's maquillage an awe-inspiring
sight), although Garbo perhaps wishes it would. If that's
what she hopes for, she has only to accept a lifetime achievement award — with retrospective, star-studded gala at Lin-
coln Center and supper afterward at Tavern on the Green —
to do the trick.

The view that Garbo would lose her glamour (retroactive
to 1926) by making such an appearance — particularly if she
dressed up for it — may not be shared by all. Many may
believe such a public display could only enhance and revi-
talize her glamour. In fact, the Joan Collins gang no doubt
would challenge my fitness to denigrate the new and improved Garbo.

True, I was not raised with luxe ("Mr. Porter's playing the
piano for Mommy, Mr. Cocteau's chatting with Daddy, I'm
playing backgammon with Peggy Guggenheim, and we're all
in her spiffing Venetian palazzo for the Easter hols"). True,
I cannot claim to hobnob with the prominent — off with
Sting to the rain forest; putting the Grimaldi sisters up when
they're in New York. But I submit that the privilege of the

former could have made me hidebound — my ideas on glamour unchanged from the time Patou designed the layette for my crib — and that exposure to the latter could have made me timid — afraid to call Monte Carlo shoddy, or cast doubt on the glamour of the Sting expedition, lest he not invite me next time.

Now, Diana Vreeland *has* enjoyed all the advantages denied me. So if she says the duchess of Windsor was one of the world's most glamorous women, her opinion is based on firsthand knowledge that, undoubtedly, colors her judgment. Even though the duchess is dead, if Diana thought her as jumped-up as Sylvester Stallone, would she dare say it?

That thought was on my mind when I went to interview her. How much, I wondered, had Diana's glamorous life stunted her ability to recognize real glamour in others? It was not a question I was tempted to voice (put it down to cowardice), so I stayed on safer ground, urging Ms. V to share reminiscences with my radio audience. "When I visited William Randolph Hearst, he lined up his zebras to greet me. They were all old and mangy — one died in the line," she was saying, when she noticed my hat, which I'd removed and put on the floor before she came into the room. Reaching down for it, she pronounced: "This hat is marvelous."

Holding it up, she identified it: "Straw . . ." Twirling it in her fingers, she studied it further. "It's the . . . ," she searched, ". . . it's that quality . . ." She examined it intently, finally deciding, "Yes . . . it's the absolute glamour of it."

"It's mine," I proclaimed.

She did not comment. Handing me the hat, she abruptly returned to the subject of William Randolph Hearst (". . . he only kept the grass-eating animals; the ones who ate meat were shipped off to the San Francisco Zoo . . ."). She avoided further discussion of my millinery (picked off a thrift table, incidentally), probably to prevent my leading off the radio spot: "Yesterday, I found myself, along with such legends as Daisy Fellowes, Maria Callas, Princess Yousoupoff, Vicomtesse de Noailles, and Babe Paley, called glamorous by none other than Diana Vreeland. And since I am in no position to pressure Ms. Vreeland into such a judgment, it seems reasonable to assume that I, alone among this glittering pantheon, truly deserve it."

Well, Ms. Vreeland need have had no such fears. My report mentioned the fact that she thought the hat was glamorous, but didn't presume she extended the description to me. A woman of such influence is in no position to make such an eccentric choice.

Unlike me. And you. Both of us, free from the fear of offending the rich and famous or annoying the media and entertainment interests, can label glamorous whomever we damn well please. Let them splutter: "You can't have everyone deciding who is glamorous!" And coolly respond: "Why not?"

It's easy enough to dismiss those standardized, all-purpose specimens of glamour like Vanna White, Nancy Reagan, Ivana Trump; but what of Bill Blass, Paloma Picasso, Jerry Hall, whose pretensions to glamour evoke classier endorsements? Can these glitterati be rejected? The answer is yes! And, moreover, they should be if they do not cause the hairs to rise on the back of your neck and shivers to run up and down your spine.

"Am I bewitched by this person?" is what you should ask yourself — because once upon a time, glamour was called "grammar" and was applied to those people who practiced the occult. In other words, to people who could cast spells, who were magical. I see you, armed with this knowledge, flinging aside the airbrushed magazine spread as you scoff: "'Glamour'! That's not the word I'd use to describe her — she couldn't charm a false promise out of a politician."

You have no idea how powerful, how independent, how satisfied you will feel, particularly if you inspire others to adopt your rebellious attitude. Express it often enough and you will.

Imagine, people everywhere speaking out on what's got them bewitched and making the image makers — always so certain of what we will accept — bothered and bewildered by our choices. Imagine their canned and packaged propositions laughed to scorn. There's no telling where such a movement would end. But where better than with glamour to begin?

The Picnic Papers

Couples can blunder on for years sensing something is wrong with their marriage but never be provided with the precise situation to bring the problem into focus.

That situation, in my case, was the picnic.

I had somewhat misrepresented myself to my future husband. I knew he was keen on nature, so I pretended to be, too. It wasn't a total deception. I really was eager to be part of the trendy back-to-nature movement. Not that I had ever been there in the first place; I grew up in London, where the great outdoors is the crowded seaside.

Because of my upbringing, I didn't have the same sense of urgency about the wilderness that my husband did. He lived in a state of anxiety that he wouldn't get the best of it before it was spoiled. Well, I thought, one spoiled nature by putting up a factory, not a soft-drink stand. My husband deplored such conveniences. His idea of the perfect picnic site was the untamed spot far from the steaming hot dog. Since there are many highway rest areas with nothing more than picnic tables and garbage cans set against a backdrop of vast tracts of forest, I thought they offered the perfect retreat for the tailgate blowout.

But he'd have none of it. Parking the car, miles from anywhere, we would beat our way through the bush toward a body of water (sometimes we found it, sometimes we didn't); once settled, my husband bustled about killing things and picking wild vegetables and fruit. I suppressed my shudders as the leaping trout was tossed into the frying pan, and never expressed my fear that the wild mushroom I nibbled on could be my last.

Though my husband's heart leapt at the sight of deer droppings and the cry of the loon, my nerves were set on edge whenever something slithered in the grass or fluttered out of a bush. Nothing irritated him quite so profoundly as my nervous starts. And after a few years, his interest in transforming me into a hardy lass capable (if cold cuts were left behind) of baking a porcupine in its own quills began to weaken.

Still, as an ardent conservationist, he was bent on preserving the marriage, so we affected a compromise: I would bring boxes of industrially fried chicken and serve it with a dandelion-and-sorrel salad and the children would pick blueberries to scatter over the commercial cheesecake.

Their father considered them heavily influenced by me. He would try to counteract it by introducing them to birdwatching; but if they failed to spot the Baltimore oriole as speedily as they picked out *Happy Days* on TV, they would pretend they'd seen it so they could get back to their comic books.

The end of our marriage possibly came when, still hoping that I would help out with woodland lore, my husband told the children to enlist my help in weaving grass place mats and they said I couldn't because I was painting my nails. Shortly thereafter, he initiated divorce proceedings and served me with picnic papers, citing my inability to build a campfire and toast a marshmallow as a major cause of marital breakdown.

We've been divorced for some time now, and I dine alfresco in my own way. I seek out dappled shade, grass, and the sun dancing off the water, all of which are to be found in Riverside Park, not a block from where I live in Manhattan.

Last time we picnicked there, I removed my daughter's headset for a moment to point out the charming sight of a squirrel chewing on a nut and watching us eat our pizza. I wish my ex could have seen how much more relaxed this little chap was than those edgy creatures of the wilderness, how harmoniously he fitted into his surroundings. My daughter looked closer.

"That's not a nut, it's a cigar butt," she said.

Even better, I thought.

Sleeping with the Boss

I knew a girl who claimed she had slept with Lord Beaverbrook when she was a hotel stenographer. The legend was that he summoned her to take dictation and, smitten, soon after gave her the rather impressive diamond ring she always wore and invited her to spend her vacations with him on his yachts and in his villas.

I could never buy the story. If it were true, why did she always return to her dreary job as an assistant buyer? Surely the rewards for sleeping with a press baron included not just jewels and holidays but *opportunities.*

While I was a typist at *The Observer* in London, I used to dream that the owner, the honorable David Astor, would be toppled by my charms . . .

"I could make you overnight," he would declare. And having done so, he would set me up in a Mayfair flat, which I would rarely inhabit because I'd be dashing about the globe as the paper's leading foreign correspondent.

Nothing of the sort happened, which is why I am writing this now, instead of busying myself with our memoirs.

Kay Summersby wrote her memoirs. She was Ike's chauffeur during World War II, but failed to drive him to matrimony after it was over. Ike went back to the wife — did Mamie even know he'd left? — and made *her* first lady.

The earl of Essex shared the Virgin Queen's bed in peace and war, but earned her displeasure on a number of counts, including his failure to put down a rebellion in Ireland and, worse, inciting one of his own. The queen had his head cut off.

Cutting off is what Somerset Maugham did to his daughter, Liza, when he tried to adopt his secretary Alan Searle and make him his heir instead. Alan might have found himself smothering under all those lovely royalties, but the courts defeated Maugham's adoption attempts and Alan had to be satisfied with a trust fund, like his predecessor, Gerald Haxton.

Valerie Fletcher, T. S. Eliot's secretary, may not have been expecting love and marriage (she worked for Tom for eight years and he was too shy to find out if she even liked him), but she got it. Valerie, cozy as a nanny, softened Tom's flinty heart, and instead of dictating to her during the day, he told her bedtime stories at night, reading aloud from Edward Lear or Kipling's *Kim*.

Few of us are as lucky as Valerie; but, given the problems of getting ahead on one's own gifts, I still think that sleeping with the boss is a good idea.

I encountered it in the very first job I had. I was a messenger, along with a handsome cockney boy named Ernie. We were both lazy, cheeky, and incompetent; but I was cleverer than he, so it came as a shock when he, not I, was promoted to junior clerk by our supervisor, a large and lugubrious blond named Renée.

"Her husband doesn't understand her," Ernie said, explaining in detail how he had stayed late and made up for that shortcoming on the camp cot kept in our quarters as part of the firm's first-aid equipment.

"You're nothing but a tart, Ernie," I told him, but that was the first and last time I expressed disapproval of such a liaison, and then only because I was so directly affected.

In my next job, I knew advancement would be as slow as my typing speed unless I adopted Ernie's fast ways. What I hoped to gain was rank over Miss Phipps, who'd been with the firm twenty years and who daily brought egg-and-cress sandwiches for her lunch so she wouldn't interrupt the flow of work by leaving her desk. She was the main obstacle to my two-hour lunches, private calls, and the right to paint my nails when things were slow. I had to go over her head and did it by fixing my employer, a weedy solicitor, with a seductive look whenever our eyes met.

On one occasion, he asked irritably: "What is the matter, Miss Garmaise? Are you ill?"

The fact that he'd failed to recognize I was giving him the eye proved that his knowledge of women was slight and that he'd be a pushover for a sixteen-year-old sexpot such as myself.

Seeing the subtle approach was useless, I was bent on bold measures and simply flung my arms around his neck when he called me into his office to thank me for taking his shoes to the menders (he'd given up asking me to type briefs).

"Miss Phipps," he screamed. And brushing wisps of cress from her lips, she rushed to his side and pried me off. I was fired on the spot.

What I failed to realize was that the reckless, romantic

gesture, which would be breathtaking strategy in other circumstances, didn't go down well in an office where impulsiveness was not admired.

Later, I again learned it is often wise to keep a leash on your appetites in front of the boss until you are quite sure they are appropriate. Invited to lunch with a fellow reporter by the editorial director, I saw the occasion as the chance for a blowout (in those days, smart lunchers had martinis, shrimp cocktails, steak with the trimmings, and strawberry cheesecake). My colleague, on the other hand, a natural-power luncher decades ahead of her time, delicately nibbled on a salad. My mouth was too full to advance my career, but no such impediment restricted her: after the lunch, she was made an associate editor, while I remained a reporter second class.

In fact, I dropped to third class. And the ironic thing is that I was the one who was sleeping with the boss. During this fling, I not only saw others promoted instead of me, but also noticed that my working conditions worsened: the boss felt that if he gave me privileged treatment, he would attract suspicion and hostility from the rest of the staff.

I always saw my affair with the man who ultimately became my ex-husband as one that belongs in the sleeping-with-the-boss category, even though he wasn't my boss. But he was on a higher level than me and that kind of distinction existed between us.

I was a fashion writer by this time and, in my snappy Saint Laurent's, a figure of sparkling glamour compared to his wife, who spent a lot of time stripping down farmhouse antiques in clothes not likely to be ruined by the odd splash of varnish remover.

I look back on that period as the most romantic of my

life. Is there anything to beat the poem in the interoffice envelope, the hands that meet under the table at the editorial meetings, the stolen moments behind filing cabinets, the out-of-town rendezvous? There was just no place for us to go but to the altar. Besides, I had seen too many movies on the subject not to know I'd never find fulfillment as a woman until I was a full-time wife and mother.

Domesticity turned me into more of a slattern than my ex-rival, who had, at least, a rocking chair or a dresser to show for her unkempt condition. Better results, I had to concede, than the unruly babies I produced, who threw up on me and dulled my intellect. My husband never let a day go by without commenting on how unappetizing I had become and expressing his amazement that I couldn't manage to be groomed and ready for bed at midnight, which was when he now chose to come home from work.

When I met his assistant, I understood why. She called him her "mentor" and I instantly knew they were sleeping together. There is a type of woman who bestows titles like that on a man to distract him from the fact that she could teach him a thing or two.

Bobbi — let's call her that — was all the inspiration I needed for the old ambitions to surface: to get out of my marriage, back into the work force, and find a boss to sleep with myself.

As a free-lance publicist, I did receive an invitation from one of my clients, who said that in exchange for a weekend in Miami I could make free use of his credit cards on Collins Avenue. I would have done it, but a chance to golf in Bermuda came up and he took that instead. He might have made me another offer, but I did so poorly publicizing his fun furs (they weren't very amusing), he soured on the idea.

Although the years have undoubtedly brought a diminishment of my charms, I like to believe that it is because I work at home (except when I go out to broadcast) that I have had no further opportunities to engage in office liaisons.

Perhaps there haven't been that many even for those in the workaday world. I have a feeling that since the period during the sixties when miniskirts brought out crotch watchers to thrill to the careless squat at the filing cabinet, there's been a decline in the office as sexual arena, and that offering the body along with the typing skills isn't the enticement it once was.

But with the current sexual retreat and uneasiness about seeking excitement in places where they don't keep files, such as singles bars and topless clubs, the nine-to-five carnal escapade with chances for advancement could soon be back, stronger than ever.

I can see *Cosmo,* ever alert to such trends, counseling its Girls on how to climb the corporate ladder by falling into bed ("Fake orgasm if you must — this *is* your career").

Given my low rate of success, it isn't likely anyone would take advice from me, and I haven't much to give beyond don't confide in anyone else on the staff (even if she does look like Thelma Ritter); cultivate an atmosphere of fear (I spoiled my chances by being foolishly reassuring); and always act as if your life is as free as his is restricted (by both his executive and domestic responsibilities). Don't look wistful on Friday nights, look expectant. A simple "Thank God it's Friday" could have him offering you a vice-presidency on Monday.

Of course, you will always feel, if you do hit the heights, that you could have done it on your talents alone. But there will be those who will insist you did it by sleeping with the boss.

One will be my aunt, who cannot contemplate the success of any woman — Jeane Kirkpatrick, Joan Collins, Madonna, Meryl Streep, Simone de Beauvoir, or Margaret Thatcher — without remarking, "Well, we all know how *she* got to the top."

I like to nurse such illusions, too, dwelling on the spectacle of Margaret Thatcher, for example — at the start of her career, after a brisk frisk with the local Conservative Party bigwig, wriggling into her two-way stretch and snapping: "And now, Nigel, here's how *I* see the party hierarchy."

The Cosmetic Commitment

The customer is perched on the stool at the cosmetic counter, the fur sliding from her shoulders. There is a sense of communion between her and the salesgirl who produces *le pot*, reverently removes the lid, slides her finger over the glossy surface, and, taking the hand of the customer, anoints the back of it with the celery whip revitalizer.

Before it is finally bought, it will be smelled and felt, its promise discussed, and the sparseness of application weighed against the extravagance of cost. This is the cosmetic commitment at work. A commitment undertaken by those women who have mercilessly looked themselves in the face and decided something can, and indeed must, be done. To this end, the cosmetically committed tirelessly practice technique with the blushes and shadows, the pick-me-ups and gloss-me-offs for every mood and outfit.

From the try-this-simple to the ten-day-miracle-turn-around test, she is at the scientists' disposal. The rat may prove the extract harmless, but only she can show if it's effective. She is a willing volunteer, eager to experiment with the nouveau crème, nouveau gel, nouveau mousse — much of it priced only within the means of the nouveau riche. Who else will be able to afford it when we get the out-of-this-world breakthrough? When the findings about gravity's pull on human skin in outer space are put to real use by the boys at the beauty clinic, who will use the data to counteract downward drift by offering us an antiaging molecule, the cost of which will run into the thousands — money the cosmetically committed will not hesitate to spend. Not for them, the wait until the latest rejuvenator turns up in a see-through, shrink-wrap pack at the discount drugstore.

I once flew to Paris with a cosmetically committed woman. She was a fashion buyer, and no sooner were we aloft than she clicked open her case — not, as I had expected, to review her buying strategy, but to work out with the dozens of remedies and revitalizers (Swiss granola scrub, Baden-Baden spa astringent — classy stuff) that were in it. She cleaned, massaged, and polished, all the while delivering lectures to me on tax reform, the descent of John Travolta, and possible uses for nuclear waste.

I was appalled. I had always comforted myself with the thought I had grown up with: that you couldn't be serious about scarlet lipstick *and* W. H. Auden. Out of that conditioning had grown the conviction that the cure for cancer would not be found by a woman wearing eyeliner. And even if it were, she wouldn't be wearing it *well*. She would be wearing it as I wear it. Carelessly. The sort of makeup job that says: I use cosmetics, but I am not obsessed with them; if necessary, I can put lipstick on without a mirror; I've got better things to think about than contouring.

But here was this woman on the plane with her cultivated chat. I had the sickening realization that if I gave as much thought to what I put on my face as I do to what I put in my stomach — if the tray in front of *me* had held astringents and mineral water instead of airline food and all those little bottles of wine — I'd be arriving at Orly as she ultimately did: having conquered jet lag with her bracers and glossers, she looked as fresh as this season's newly picked *pêche*.

Beside her, I was as stale and uninviting as my soiled makeup bag. I hadn't dared to bring it out in front of her, so before we landed I went to the lav to repair the ravages. But after I scratched myself on the wood of the worn-down eyeliner pencil, crushed my blusher when I dropped the case on the floor, and found I'd forgotten to take my moisturizer from the side of my bathroom sink, I just gave up.

It's times like these when the thought is driven home that girls are making themselves up even for the big jobs. Not just Diane Sawyer, but the head of state she interrogates — all glossy grooming from her tippy toes to the marcelled waves of her Thatch (how *very* Norma Shearer, Margaret).

It's hard to believe bankers and psychiatrists and activists are all doing it: fussing over shade cards and ordering the new mocha glaze lip gloss by phone. It always seemed so shallow to fuss — apart from being an admission that you really needed it and didn't have the looks to get away with lipstick and mascara applied indifferently.

But even the greatest beauties care, and although they regularly reveal their secrets ("I happen to have a glorious complexion and I keep it that way by drinking ten glasses of water a day"), I know I'll never learn anything from them.

I think I could benefit if I could sidle up to the cosmetics counter computer, feed my face into it, and then keep the findings to myself. But I know there is someone waiting to snatch the printout and scream, "Boy, take a look at these pores. Talk about stressed!"

That is why my admiration is boundless for the brave girl who publicly parks herself in the department store aisle and submits to the cosmetologist, crowded in by that little knot of women who gather round to pick up info while someone else is the stooge.

We all need help. And I'm not going to get it from the girl at the discount shop, who never ventures an opinion as to whether the Midnight Smudgeproof or the Mink Brown Magi-Lash will best bring out my eyes. She seems interested only in taking my money and barking, "Next!"

It is her curt dismissal that makes me easy game for the fawning hypocrite who accosts me as I examine the shades at the cosmetics counter. "It's not for everyone," he assures me, "but *you* can take our new Sage 'n' Blush series."

And take it I do, enthusiastically accepting the notion that this new color scheme can be shown to advantage only on a person of my rare qualities. It is then impossible to withdraw my offer on the grounds of cost. Only after I am blushed, glossed, and shaded does the extent of my folly sink in: I have used the housekeeping money to look like a ruddy version of Morticia.

But these mistakes are inevitable from someone whose last serious commitment to cosmetics was when the makeup men were saying, "Pledge to me only with thine eyes." Which I thought was terrific advice. I'd always thought lips — continually engaged in talking, eating, licking, biting, kissing — were far too active for the trouble-free cosmetic statement. Eyes, on the other hand, seemed unlikely to be disturbed, apart from the odd tear, and were a much better spot. To this day, I still list eyeliner as the most indispensable item in the makeup kit. I went all out when eyes came in, wearing gobs of mascara and thickly applied liner. My feeling was that what I lacked in skill I could compensate for with excess.

Now, as the years jog on, I wonder: can age be avoided? Yes, the beauty boys say, but it won't happen overnight. Meanwhile, just keep on using the moisturizer (never mind that Bianca Jagger has stopped), get on with active cell renewal (passive cell renewal, if you want to sleep through it), take a close-up look at the rejuvenators, and investigate tucks and lifts.

The trouble with being alive, they point out, is that we just don't seem to be able to do it without registering our reactions and emotions. As a result, our skin suffers from the punishment inflicted by the daily round of expressions that assault the features.

If only one could have the complexion that cloistering gives, without the life. Is it so farfetched to think of nuns (or monks, for that matter) taking part in face tests to see if the rest of the world couldn't have the same serene, creaseless skin they enjoy? Could their glands have been innocently secreting something all these centuries — let's call it monasterium ad tedium — that could be duplicated for the benefit of all mankind?

I know I should commit myself *now* to the youth mousse extracted by some Romanian rejuvenator, but I worry. Supposing it does plump out my flesh, but also swells my joints? What if I find myself to be a fresh-faced beauty at sixty, but also knobbed and gnarled with arthritis?

But then, there's always some niggling question. Just

when I've decided, once and for all, that I am definitely going for the all-out commitment of a Linda Evans, I see Jessica Lange and Vanessa Redgrave, who wear makeup for work only — and not even then, if the part doesn't call for it — and I'm thrown.

And I think, "Oh, it's *so* Pat Buckley to go crazy over your looks," and *then* I think of Lena Horne and Louise Nevelson and I get uneasy as I toy with the idea that they must have been having their cells renewed for years and it's probably too late now, anyway.

In my panic, I rush at the moisturizer and apply it as thickly as I once saw Charlie Chaplin do when he removed his makeup as a broken-down actor in *Limelight*. (Right there, the character didn't work for me; how come he could use all that cold cream if he was so poor?)

I suppose my commitment to cosmetics will go on being light except for my heavy hand with the eyeliner — which once brought me to the attention of a beauty editor, who thought its excessive use made me a perfect candidate for a make-over. But I've always hated make-overs. Better to look unkempt and interesting than groomed and boring. So I turned her down.

"My makeup might not be perfect but it reflects the real me," I said.

"Precisely," she agreed.

Perhaps if I had been made over, I would never have been overdone again. Yet I don't regret my decision. To me, the prime-time blonds, each a Morgan Fairchild clone, look like make-overs, and I have no wish to project their standardized allure. You'll never mistake me for the one in the sitcom. Perhaps you wish you could. But it is *my* face. You might have to look at it. But *I* have to live with it.

An Ardent Spirit

As a silly, immature drinker, who has neither the nose nor the palate to acquire a buzz in a classy way, I find that vodka is perfect for me. It gives a satisfactory zap, and once mixed with juice, loses its medicinal bite.

My drinking habits are the result of a background of heavy Irish and light Russian drinkers. My father never tried vodka. I doubt many Jews of his generation did. The very word must have struck terror: "Vodka!" one could hear the cossacks scream, sufficiently inflamed by it to swoop down on the shtetl.

Russians have been drinking themselves insensible on vodka for eight hundred years, but occasionally a man of moderation comes along, becomes a connoisseur, and comes to America to show us how to drink it properly. I met one who said vodka should be taken "neat" — thrown down the throat as if it were Jell-O — and followed by a nosh. I don't intend to try it. I have no wish to improve myself as a drinker.

I am already the despair of those who urge moderation, especially those who warn against the evils of drinking alone. I am never *happier* than when drinking alone. There is nothing to be compared to a vodka with juice — any juice — to banish the cares of the day, bring a rapturous appetite to the makeshift meal ahead, and even incite an imitation of Cyd Charisse dancing on the MGM soundstage.

When drinking in company, such an impulse must be stifled, and one must also know how to toy with a drink. I don't. I guzzle at the outset, then lose interest and want to go home.

My Irish grandfather would have disapproved. Starting with whiskey to wash down his morning kippers, he practiced what he believed: that alcohol as a constant companion rounds out a man. The term *alcohol abuse* wasn't around then, but Grandfather would have thought that the way I drink — zapping myself with fortified fruit juice — or the way Dad did — spluttering over the odd schnapps — would have merited the term.

Or perhaps he wouldn't. Since he considered only whiskey worth drinking, he probably would have thought vodka and schnapps were getting the treatment they deserved. If he were around today to hear about the latest blow life has dealt me, I know what he'd say as he grimaced with distaste over the screwdriver I gave him: "You can't expect to get the best out of life if you don't get into the right spirit."

Tune In, Turn Up ... Turn On?

"Turn that woman off!" a man used to say whenever I came on the radio. When told this, I felt uneasy, and then sympathetic. After all, I am a listener too, and I make good on my word when I snap at a radio voice, "You're not taking that tone with me!" In fact, appalled at my unctuousness in a taped exchange with Jessica Lange, I once switched *myself* off.

Radio, as Marshall McLuhan pointed out, is a hot medium: the listener and broadcaster are heavily engaged with each other. The extent to which the broadcaster enters the lives of some listeners can be gauged by a friend of mine, who, pitched into gloom over a positive pregnancy test, flung a book at the radio, shouting: "Thanks very much, Garrison Keillor, and now go fuck yourself."

When the Canadian Broadcasting Corporation was airing my radio commentaries, I was not immune from listeners taking out their troubles on me. I was once accosted by a woman whose husband had died of a heart attack: "When we found him, the radio was on, and you were carrying on about Elliott Gould," she said reproachfully.

Such experiences deter me from holding those *I* regularly listen to responsible for my unpaid bills. In fact, the people I listen to on radio are one of my main sources of distraction from such sordid trifles. They take my mind off my problems by reminding me of the large events in life.

As a broadcaster, I was meant to perform a similar function for the listener, but in reverse. In my reviews and commentaries, I dealt with the lighter side. I was expected to confine my remarks to Ingmar Bergman and to stay away from really serious matters like the sanitary workers' strike.

"There is nothing funny about garbage," my producer said, reducing my script on the subject to confetti and tossing it into the trash can (where it would not be picked up for weeks). There was airtime to be filled, so I spoke on streaking instead. I argued that this latest craze was actually a regressive reaction to all the prolonged nudity we were being treated to in the movies, and that its peekaboo quality gave us the chance to rediscover the charm of the unexpected and fleeting exposure. The public outrage that greeted this suggestion far exceeded any outcry that would have been provoked by the initial topic, "What You Can Do with Your Garbage" (forecast the future with chicken bones). Furious listeners demanded to know why their taxes were being spent by the CBC, a federally funded agency, on perverted broadcasters who actively encouraged flashers.

Since those concerned with news and public affairs are apt to look down on do-gooders as people who lack serious stature, they didn't see any risk in their decision to send me to interview a woman who was righting wrongs throughout the world under the auspices of the United Nations. It so happened that she regularly wore a uniform reminiscent of Lady Mountbatten's wartime rig.

As I sat before the studio mike during a break, waiting to deliver my live introduction of the taped interview, I confided to the program's host that the uniform gave a slightly ridiculous and pompous cast to this estimable woman; the host asked if I had reacted to her as I might to "Hot Lips" Houlihan, a character on *M*A*S*H*. With that thought in my mind, I heard my cue and said on the air: "Tirelessly kiss crossing the globe . . ." Seized with giggles, I managed to infect the host, who also found herself incapable of salvaging the situation. This disgraceful behavior might have ruined us both, had not the producer segued to music, swearing to herself that I would never again be allowed to interrogate anyone more important than the man who was giving a course on witchcraft at a local community college.

The day I was on campus to conduct that interview, one of the sons of Ethel and Julius Rosenberg turned up on a speaking tour and decided this was the moment to accuse the prosecuting attorney at his parents' trial of perjuring himself. Word spread that there was a reporter from CBC around, and I got a scoop. The news people were impressed, and despite my past misdemeanors, there was some talk of having me do more serious stuff because of my ability to get people to talk. But the truth was that the Rosenberg *fils* had volunteered his information — in fact, he'd urged it on me, and seemed taken aback when I said he could rely on me to respect his confidence if he wished to withdraw it.

I gave Sophia Loren the same option when she confided in me that she always slept with the light on. While my producer in the control room frantically shook her head and her fists, I remarked to Sophia: "That's rather intimate — would you like it deleted from the tape?"

I might be far richer than I am if I'd encouraged such revelations (since they could also be peddled elsewhere); but whenever I suspected a subject's guard was coming down, I would nervously try to shore it up, convinced that intimate detail was none of my business. Who knows what confessions might have been rising to the lips of Tom Hanks had I not prevented him from saying something he might regret later? When I got back to the studio after that interview, my producer listened to the tape and said: "I already know your top-ten comedy hits and your feelings about sitcoms, and I have heard that story about you, the boa constrictor, and Dom DeLuise a hundred times — what did Mr. Hanks have to say for himself?"

On such occasions, it has been implied that I hogged the mike because I felt myself to be as much in the star milieu as the celebrity under interrogation. Well, I suppose there have been times when I have been guilty of that, particularly when I've tried to project myself as "a personality."

As a listener, however, I harbor a different philosophy: the less personality the broadcaster has, the better. I want him to deliver his opinions without those assumptions of gravity, ironic inflections, sarcastic asides, and so on that I can add for myself at the Saturday-night dinner party when I repeat his views on how the sunken fortunes of coal and railroads have molded the political outlook of small-town America.

Talk radio — not the abusive phone-in sort, but the type where we hear thoughtful ruminations on the impact of noiseless Velcro on the military — is what I tune to until, sick of the sound of it all, I switch to bands and singers. This defection never lasts long ("Go and *ask* how much that doggie is, Patti!"), and I soon turn the dial back to where music merely bridges the items — a mariachi band playing me into a piece on Mexico's *Day of the Dead,* a few bars on the clavichord conditioning me for the political discussion. The kind of ratio, when all is said and done, that I know and love best.

Just the same, when I started in radio after working as a print journalist, I was unaware of its powerful reach. I can remember being totally taken aback when I was approached by a man at a party who told me, "I listen to you all the time."

"Then I'd better watch what I say," I said nervously.

I meant it. Up until that moment, I had never mentally linked myself at the mike to this man at his drawing board — he was a commercial artist — or to listeners anywhere else, for that matter.

An apologetic air crept into my broadcasts. I started to qualify everything I said and I grew more and more insipid, until finally my producer complained. When I confessed to the source of the problem, she advised: "Never, ever, think of the listener. That awareness has ruined more broadcasters than anything else."

I have never forgotten this dictum, and can honestly say that I have never placed myself in front of the mike since without heeding its wisdom.

A Certain Age

When Cher said she hated being forty, I wasn't surprised. Her high-wire style can't help but be undermined by that caution that is bound to creep in as the years go by.

Given her outlook, it's no wonder she looks so wearied in those health club commercials. It's as if she is thinking that all the years of grueling gymnastics will bring, in the long run, is the cruel reminder that even if she has the body of a twenty-four-year-old, she isn't one. Cher gives the impression that she doesn't want to look good *in spite* of her age, she wants to forget it. And she wants us to forget it.

The only way we can all do that is if she becomes a woman of a certain age — a woman of beauty and mystery who doesn't aspire to be youthful and who, if anything, *emphasizes* her ripeness to show how callow and raw anyone younger is by comparison.

France used to turn out women of a certain age like America turned out wisecracking girl Fridays — but the chattering printout has replaced the latter and aerobics (after all, the French work out, too) has rendered the woman of a certain age all but extinct. Cher could revive her. She should shed her biker lady image and her curly-haired rock star image and start conducting life from a divan. She has the beauty, the sophistication, the wit, the *langueur* for it, and I'm betting in no time at all would find herself mentioned in the same breath as the immortals — Pompadour, Maintenon, Edwige Feuillère — whose age was the least of their statistics.

If Cher has to find a new style to grow old in, the one Diane Keaton has will do nicely. Diane can rumble around in her roomy Yamamotos (or something equally unorthodox) until she's ninety. Her avant-garde style, coupled with a penchant for eccentric concealment — mittens, tights for the beach, hats worn low on the brow — is more rejuvenating than a face-lift. Diane could outwit age as successfully as did Andy Warhol, who was ever the wunderkind with his farmboy thatch. Andy's look was so successful that when he died and it was revealed that he was fifty-nine, people were shocked. "It's gross. He was going to Tunnel and everything and he was, like, this old guy," a teenage friend of my daughter's complained, smarting from *her* exclusion from the place.

To be ruled out on the basis of age is something Dianne Wiest is trying to avoid, if her refusal to tell hers to the *New York Times* is anything to go by. Dianne is a late starter, but you have to be *really* late, like Grandma Moses or Colonel Sanders, for age to be an asset. For anyone else, no matter how glittering the belated debut, prospective employers are likely to think: "So what if audiences like her? So what if she gets great reviews? So what if she won the Academy Award? How come she didn't make it before now?"

You'd think the example of Joan Collins, who became a

sex goddess thirty years after she first applied for the job, would put an end to such carping. But Joan — like the eleven-year-old girl who became a grandmother — has that *National Enquirer* freak appeal. Still, she ought to be ready to chance it. If she stays in her present groove, her future could be a tawdry one, starring in movies scripted by sister Jackie (from the early works) in which Joan plays a temptress who seduces schoolboys. Much better for her to turn herself into an icon (she's almost there) and become the successor to Mae West.

Not everyone can become an icon and many stars are discovering that the next-best thing is to get yourself reborn. By doing so, you can escape the stigma of becoming old due to the shameful passage of time and blame drugs and drink for it. Even if it isn't true. Simply succumbing to rejuvenating surgery is . . . well, it *isn't* inspirational. It isn't movie-of-the-week stuff. An addiction to vodka and Valium *is* — and since the public is naive enough to believe that just giving it up makes you look younger, then why not take advantage of it? Look at Elizabeth Taylor: whatever restoration she has undergone is ignored by the media and instead we are given to understand it's her recovery from alcohol and drugs that alone is responsible for her new, miraculous bloom of youth.

Thousands of women give up drinking and taking drugs, but they don't look any younger for it. Even those who have led blameless lives, with scarcely an indulgence beyond chocolate and Bingo, end up looking older than those who can afford to repair the effects of years of dissipation with the spa and the surgeon's knife. Perhaps the unfairness of it all will be remedied if face-lifts get cheaper. Then looking old will be just another disadvantage of being poor, and will perhaps be seen as a sign of weakness and failure, as being fat is today.

The cosmetics companies are capitalizing on this fear — and on the fact that everyone is turning forty — by turning out antiaging products as fast as they can think up names and claims. Adrien Arpel is the most ingenious, with Line Fill, which she calls "a spackle," after the stuff you put in the cracks before painting. Imagine what Line Fill could have done for W. H. Auden, who had a face like a dry riverbed and may have been resigned to it if

> *Oh let not time deceive you*
> *You cannot conquer time . . .*

is anything to go by. No such considerations stay Arpel, who briskly counsels the use of her skin spackle to "fill in those character lines we can do without."

With crow's-feet, laugh lines, and frown furrows smoothed away, you can always *tell* people you've lived — although many won't want to and will guard against spoiling the effectiveness of the cellular wrinkle crème by looking mystified when the hula hoop or Van Cliburn are mentioned.

It's too bad that character lines leave such an unflattering impression. Many of the elderly, for instance, look down-in-the-mouth when they are really quite cheerful. As a result, we tend to ignore them for fear they'll be as dreary as their expression promises. A lift could put on a happy face and give them the chance to show what an amusing and diverting lot they really are. On the other hand, if the face does mirror the disposition, it could be deeply frustrating to be given a carefree kisser only to find that a lifetime's aggravation was no longer taken seriously.

Keeping up appearances is an exhausting business, and if

there is one advantage to growing old, it is that you no longer have to bother and are content to be prized, if at all, for your experience and wisdom alone.

Such credentials may not be sufficient in the future, when rows of girls routinely tuck back skin as they now push back cuticles, and the wise old granny is replaced by the smart-ass Golden Girl.

Will it mean that those who are stuck with looking old will just look old and vacant, old and stupid, old and uninteresting? And will we have seen the last of the great ancient faces like those of an Einstein or a Colette?

Colette was deeply aware of her appearance throughout her life (she once ran her own cosmetics company), even though she looked her age for all of it. It didn't seem to matter. In her sixties, stout and with frizzy hair, her allure was powerful enough for Maurice Goudeket, who had courted her for ten years, to count himself lucky to make her his wife. Truman Capote met her when she was in her seventies and said she had a face as "mobile as water" — a quality, incidentally, a face-lift cannot often provide. Nevertheless, many people feel a certain stiffness is to be preferred if it means they won't end up looking as nature intended. Colette, of course, did end up that way — but on her it looked like a work of art.

It's depressing to think that it won't appear that way to future generations, who no doubt will look at photographs of that wondrous face and ask: "Why didn't she *do* something about herself?"

I'd Rather Be in Philadelphia

When I told my daughters I'd like to be cremated but had no plans for my ashes, they asked if I'd like them flung at someone who'd annoyed me. It seemed like a good idea at the time, but after hearing about Dorothy Parker's ashes, I am reconsidering.

Dorothy Parker wanted to be cremated but didn't leave instructions about her ashes. Apart from her legendary epitaph "Excuse My Dust," her self-effacement on the subject of death was well known, and it isn't likely she would have asked that her ashes be kept in some hallowed place or scattered on a historic, epic, or even scenic site. If pressed for a decision, she might have said, "Oh, just file them away until further notice" — which is precisely what happened.

"The least I can do is die," she remarked in her will, and she did so in 1967 at the age of seventy-four. Her ashes were kept at a mortuary in the Bronx until the proprietors complained they weren't getting storage money. The canister was then sent to Lillian Hellman, the executrix of Dorothy's will. When Lillian died, her lawyer, Oscar Bernstein, got them, and when he in turn died, they went to his partner Paul O'Dwyer. Mr. O'Dwyer is the judiciary brain behind New York City's Saint Patrick's Day parade and a man who knows how to turn a can of ashes into a public cause. He asked Liz Smith if she'd use her column to elicit suggestions for a resting place other than his filing cabinet and, on Ash Wednesday, invited some of those who responded to gather at the Algonquin and voice their ideas.

Among those who came was an actress from the Yale School of Drama who was doing a show called *Pieces of Parker* and wanted to wrap the ashes in twists of paper to distribute to her audience; a woman from Texas who felt the ashes would help her to get booked on talk shows ("Welcome, if you will, the ashes of Dorothy Parker, brought to you by . . ."; and Liz Smith, who thought they should go to the Algonquin. In the end, they went to the National Association for the Advancement of Colored People, whose president, Ben Hooks, didn't *seem* all that keen on getting them (perhaps he was thinking urn costs, pedestal, *upkeep*). Few knew that Parker left all her money to Martin Luther King, Jr., and that when he died, it went to the NAACP.

And now that her ashes are lodged in the same place, I suspect she'd be glad. Flip and dismissive about almost everything (including her own gifts), she wanted to be taken seriously when it came to issues. An active anti-Fascist and supporter of justice for blacks, she'd be overjoyed, I think, to see her remains linked in perpetuity with the latter cause, especially since she hadn't gone through the indignity of requesting it.

As a rule, Dorothy did not use her witty ways to speak up for the underdog — unless you want to count the time she met snobby, conservative Somerset Maugham, who invited her to supply two more lines to

> *Higgledy Piggledy my black hen*
> *She lays eggs for gentlemen*

and she came up with

> *You can't persuade her with gun or lariat*
> *To come across for the proletariat.*

There might be those who fear that visitors passing before Dorothy's urn at the Baltimore headquarters of the NAACP will think of her *only* as benefactress (a tricky distinction anyway) and not be aware of her as leading American wit.

But these fears will be laid to rest if the HBO movie of her life based on the biography *Dorothy Parker: What Fresh Hell Is This?* by Marion Meade gets made. Especially if it stars Holly Hunter, who turned up on Ash Wednesday — wan, fragile, *short* — the very personification of the woman who said, "I was just a little Jewish girl trying to be cute."

So, thanks to her ashes, it looks as if we're in for a full-fledged Dorothy Parker revival (a benefit in her name against illiteracy is also planned). Which is more than we would have got if she had directed that her ashes be dashed in the face of Clare Boothe Luce (the likeliest candidate, since Dorothy despised her) and the gesture had passed unnoticed, or, if the perpetrator remembered to announce it as a photo opportunity, had excited only momentary shock.

It's certainly got me thinking. I have now decided I definitely do not wish my ashes to be used for one last hostile act. Apart from the continual need to update the name of the recipient, which would be a terrible nuisance, my ashes would not then be available should there be a request from a classy source (I wouldn't rule out poets' corner in Westminster Abbey — although others would). No, I shall insist they be stored under the kitchen sink, in the broom closet, or in some equally unpretentious place. I think it pays to be unassuming about these arrangements. Look where it got Dorothy Parker.

Plain Talk about Fancy Dressers

Is it so terrible to want to wear a mountaineering outfit though you have never climbed a mountain? And never will?

Phil Donahue has permitted cross-dressers to appear on his show and press their case to wear women's clothes; might he one day give an airing to those who persist in wearing costumes that have nothing to do with their lives?

Could we one day tune in to see a woman appear in a wet suit, with tank strapped to her back, flippers on her feet, fishing spear in her hand? . . .

PHIL: You want the right to dress like that and yet you won't go near the water, right?

GUEST *(defiantly):* Why should I be deprived of the thrill of the getup because I have a horror of sinking to the depths and possibly colliding with a large and spiteful fish?

PHIL *(to the second guest, a Balinese temple dan-*

186

cer): Am I to assume that you don't dance? And that, furthermore, your name is O'Herlihy?

SECOND GUEST: That is correct.

PHIL *(to the third guest, a kilted bagpiper):* And that you can't play that thing?

THIRD GUEST: Not a note.

PHIL *(to the fourth guest, resplendent in ecclesiastical vestments):* And that you have not been ordained?

FOURTH GUEST *(waving a benediction at Phil):* That is the sacred truth, my son.

PHIL *(turning toward audience):* Okay, what if your role in life doesn't fit the clothes on your back — is it okay to wear them anyway? *(Spots a woman with raised hand and nimbly leaps to the row in which she is sitting, stretching the mike to catch her words.)*

WOMAN: No. Life is confusing enough already. I don't want the gas station attendant looking like a Balinese temple dancer.

PHIL: Why?

WOMAN: I'll think he's collecting for something *(laughter).* And that one dressed as the pope —

FOURTH GUEST: The archbishop of Canterbury, madam.

WOMAN: Whatever — is that legal?

FOURTH GUEST *(hotly, with an evangelical edge to his voice):* I'll tell you what's illegal — running some ministry racket in a three-piece suit. I don't use these clothes except to look and feel good. Is that a sin?

PHIL *(to the audience):* Well, is it? If he doesn't preach
at us or try to get money out of us *(laughter),*
where's the harm? Ever want to dress up like an
astronaut? Or a ballerina? When you're not what
you wear, who are you? Can you wear a kilt, carry
a bagpipe, and still sell insurance? We'll be back
right after these messages. Don't go away. . . .

I shan't. As a closet fancy dresser, I shall be fascinated to
see and hear those who have come out — envying them,
perhaps, and wishing I myself were on Phil's show. If I were,
I can tell you exactly what I would be wearing. A riding
habit. And since I would not be on a horse, I would have "a
beautiful seat," with my booted legs flung out nonchalantly
before me; occasionally, I would flick them with my riding
crop.

I live on Manhattan's Upper West Side, and every so often
I see people in riding habits making calls from public
phones, using ATMs, or just walking on Broadway — going
to and from the stables on Seventy-ninth Street. Or are they?
Perhaps they have no more business wearing jodhpurs than
I do. Perhaps they, too, suffer from fear of riding. Perhaps
they, too, detest horses, believing them to be high-strung
and hysterical, only too ready to misinterpret the tap on the
flank or the spur in the side and bolt, kick, or bite. Perhaps
these Broadway riders merely love the clothes.

Just like me. If I could afford it, I would be similarly at-
tired, taking my chances on being revealed as an eques-
trienne in clothes only.

It's not that I have never ridden. I have. I was once pre-
vailed upon to mount a horse named Granny, who was,
thank God, as sluggish as her name suggests. I could have

ridden her in a housedress and curlers and I would have been
appropriately turned out. But on that occasion, I was wearing jeans and sneakers.

When engaged in an outdoorsy activity — when my performance is on the line — I tend toward the nondescript outfit. It is après, as it were, that I wish to call attention to
myself, and that's when I make my debut on the deck of the
ski lodge, streamlined from boots to goggles, with a flurry of
lift tickets chicly dangling from my jacket zippers. I will
look then as if I welcome the nerve-shattering plunge down
the mountain; but when I am really skiing (if you can call
going out for a winter walk and strapping on skis so you
won't sink in the snow skiing), I avoid wearing anything
convulsive, and am indistinguishable from a rural factory
worker bundled up in a grubby parka and knitted cap as she
makes her way to the fish-canning plant.

If designers understand anything, it is the decorative appeal of active wear, and they do their best to accommodate
it by submerging the wet suit into the rubber dance dress,
for instance. But that is not what we fancy dressers require.
We need the total look.

Sometimes, the look is easy to acquire. Particularly in
professional masquerades. To appear in the hospital setting
and invite the awed glance and the whispered, "She must be
the liver specialist," you need only a lab coat and the right
expression. Since I have no idea what that expression is, I
wear my lab coat for kitchen chic.

I was wearing it the night my doctor friend Irene came to
dinner. She was so impressed to see the work garment put
to such imaginative use that she hung her stethoscope
around my neck as "the finishing touch."

"*Clinique et cuisine,*" she said, lapsing into French to

compare me with that gourmet doctor in Alice B. Toklas's cookbook who used his hypodermic syringe to inject a leg of lamb with a marinade. We weren't quite the same, I pointed out. What culinary use would I have for a stethoscope? All the ingredients for my meal were dead on arrival. "Oh, it could still be useful," she said, "*after* we've eaten."

If the need had arisen, I would have given her back the stethoscope *and* the lab coat with it. Dressing the part doesn't mean playing it. I discovered that that was something to be avoided when I was eleven and my friends and I tossed a coin to see which of the three of us would impersonate a paid-admission adult and accompany the other two into the movies for free. I lost (or won, *they* said), and in my mother's coat and a hat with a veil, I got them in to see Alan Ladd. I am sure the cashier wasn't fooled, just glad of our business on a slow day. But I was humiliated. You dressed up as a grown-up to make fun of adults or to pretend to be a movie star . . . but to be mistaken for an ordinary, mundane woman with monthlies and corsets — well, I felt as if I were choking on my mother's face powder. I couldn't wait to take the coat and hat off and be a girl again in my school uniform — which, oddly enough, was a sort of disguise, too, because as the only Jewish (or half-Jewish) girl in a WASP school, I felt it made me like the others.

This feeling persisted into weekends and holidays, but then I wore my Girl Scout outfit, which I hoped linked me directly in the eyes of the world with All Saints Church, to which our troop belonged. I went on wearing the uniform after being told I was a disgrace to it, having had the lowest standing in the matters of knots, nature study, and codes (of behavior as well as Morse) in the history of the troop.

Too bad that fitness to wear the uniform was the determining factor rather than my attraction to it. I kept my old Girl Scouts uniform long after I'd left school, and often, after a day of mindless labor in my office drabs, I would put it on. And I must say, entitled to wear it or not, that was the *only* time during that bleak period that anything I wore made me feel like myself.

Make My Taste

The other day I picked up a bran cracker sample from Sweden in a health food store and it exploded in my mouth like so much Scandinavian sawdust. Usually, though, samples taste good. Even if they don't, I always eat them as if they do — licking my fingers, smacking my lips — in case a TV crew is lurking nearby, looking for someone to deliver the glowing endorsement that will allow her to buy a yacht on the residuals.

I expect to make money from free samples, not spend it. Even so, I have a twinge of guilt when I have to face the lady in the supermarket who's handing out the sausage tidbit and garnishing it with a little promotional chat. I always respond, "I'm going to remember this," hoping she'll take it as an assurance that although I've exhausted my shopping budget for this week, her teeny wienies will be top of my list next time.

On a couple of occasions, I have bought a slab of cheese based on my enthusiasm for the store sample, only to get it home and find it tastes like soap. Do manufacturers do something to these samples to make them taste better? It is too unsettling to think marketers are that perfidious. I prefer to believe that it is a question of size: however tasteless the fish cake is in the larger quantity, in the nibble, it is tolerable.

And then, of course, the sample is free. Everything tastes better free — as my mother discovered, years ago, when she went about her housework happily munching on a chocolate bar we'd received as a sample through the mail. Later, while out shopping, she made the inconvenient discovery that it was not a candy product but a laxative. Her hostility toward the manufacturer was boundless, particularly when she checked the wrapper later and found that, indeed, flavor was stressed, while function was dealt with in fine print.

She never bought the product — joining those millions of others who prove that getting a taste of the product is not the same as getting a taste for it.

For Crying Out Loud

People talk more to themselves in New York City than they do to each other. Chatting yourself up as you go about the city is a way of keeping your wits about you, rehearsing conversations you expect to have, and reliving those that have already taken place. These solo exercises produce a continuous buzz of sound that is occasionally broken by the raised voice: "I bust my ass for you. Bust my ass! And now you're telling me you don't need me. That I'm fired. You're gonna be sorry you was ever born . . ."

These remarks addressed to the passing parade are obviously the extension of a scene that took place earlier. The speaker is simply letting off steam and, far from expecting a response, would in all likelihood be deeply shocked if someone, inspired by his belligerence, were to detach himself from the crowd and offer: "Let's go git that son of a bitch!"

Never speak when spoken to is the golden rule. The solitary talker may fancy he detects an aggressive tone if you inquire, "Are you talking to me?" — like the tone Robert

194

DeNiro adopted in *Taxi Driver* when he repeatedly asked that question while talking both to and at himself as he assessed his performance in a mirror. If you seem sufficiently menacing, the solitary talker might deny he meant you — or, feeling challenged, he may instead decide you were indeed the object of his remarks — when he looked up from rummaging through the trash can, happened to meet your eye, and said: "Filth, that's what you are, filth!"

There is always the possibility that you feel you merit such a description — what New York pedestrian isn't riddled with guilt? — in which case, a sizable donation to the talker is advised. Despite offering the handout, you may continue to be berated; you may even be accused of trying to buy off your beneficiary. Do not involve yourself in a debate. Better to go away and work for a better world, one in which grievances such as the talker's get the hearing they deserve.

It is difficult not to offer support of some kind to the man on the subway who slaps his newspaper and says, "What gives you the right? I never voted for you!" — but suppress the urge. It is true he may welcome the fact that you share his ideas on Oliver North, but he may also resent your intrusion just at the moment when he has the wretched colonel groveling at his feet.

As a public speaker, I wouldn't appreciate the casual passerby throwing in his two cents' worth on matters meant for my ears only. But there was once an occasion when I interceded in a stranger's discussion with herself — when the woman seated next to me said, "Oh, my God, the iron!"

Leaping up, I sounded the alarm: "Stop the bus! A fire! There could be a fire!"

"Okay, keep calm, folks," the driver said, trying to make his way to me as other riders made a dash for the door. "Where is it? Where?"

"In her house," I said, waving at the iron lady, who had remained in her seat, staring fixedly out the window.

"Hey, what kind of a stunt is this?" he demanded of me.

"Someone call the cops — this dame's a public nuisance," suggested one of the passengers.

"Nah, just put her off the bus, she's nuts," others chorused.

"She's left her iron on, you idiots!" I yelled as the woman, stony-faced, refused to be drawn into the altercation. "Tell them," I urged.

"I have never seen this woman before in my life," she replied.

Soliliquizers are more evident in New York because of the widespread use of public transportation and because so many people walk the streets. But all over America, people in cars and in homes and in offices are chattering away to themselves, and pretending to be singing or coughing when caught in the act. There is always the fear that if you talk to yourself in public, people will think you are crazy. Yet the madman probably believes he is not talking to himself so much as to Mussolini, and if he simultaneously entertains the delusion that he himself is Mae West, may be said to play no part in the conversation whatsoever.

Even sane people frequently talk to vending machines, toasters, and vacuum cleaners. The kitchen cupboard is sharply reprimanded when the head gets banged on it; the automated-teller machine submits to a stinging rebuke when it fails to calculate that if $700 was deposited on Tuesday, a $20 withdrawal shouldn't be too much to ask on Thursday.

The need to talk things over with yourself is never felt more sharply than when shopping. To buy, or not to buy: that is the question; and it is one of such moment that it brings out the serious soliliquizer. It is she who stands before the shelf of saucepans at Macy's saying to the beautiful but disdainful double boiler from France: "If I'm going to be treated with contempt every time I put a little cornstarch in the sauce . . ."

Should a salesclerk, overhearing such a remark, try to put the shopper's mind at rest ("These pots will make just about anyone a great cook"), he will be met with a vacant stare as she mutters, "Just looking." She will never confess: "Just talking."

It is easy to be intimidated in New York shops. This is a lox-crazed city, and to brave the fish counter at Zabar's is to reenact a run on a Shanghai bank while the invading Japanese are poised on the outskirts of the city. You will find people listing their requirements and at the same time clearly stating their rights: "A half a pound of Nova — and just because it's the cheapest smoked salmon doesn't mean I don't deserve to have it sliced very, very thinly; a quarter-pound of sable, even thinner — I know there are a hundred and eighty people waiting to be served and you only have one pair of hands, but that is your problem; a nice piece of whitefish — no, not cut from that piece, *that* piece; and two smoked trout, I'll take the one on the right, one on the *right* — look, I happen to be a regular customer; also, I have been waiting for forty-five minutes, so just get me the manager; also —"

"Number forty-eight!" a voice breaks in. "Forty-eight! Who's got number forty-eight?"

"Er . . . forty-eight . . . me . . . me, over here . . . I want . . . er . . . I think . . . er, lemme see . . ."

My married years taught me only too well that confusion is likely to strike at such a moment, even if you do engage in preliminary soliloquizing. In my private chats with myself, I would calmly point out my husband's shortcomings and calmly suggest where he could improve. Yet within seconds of actually confronting him, I would be reduced to incoherent raving.

"You don't know what you're talking about," he would say.

"I do when I'm talking to myself," I'd assure him.

"Then you'd be better off keeping your remarks to yourself. That way there will be no misunderstandings."

But chronic soliliquizers have a problem: they never know when they're running on at the mouth, which can lead them to put their foot in it. I was once a dinner party guest and the hostess boasted she'd made the pasta sauce with all-natural ingredients. What was on my mind — that she hadn't washed the fresh-picked organic basil too well — was also, unbidden, suddenly on my lips.

"Nothing like true grit," I said.

When the first thing that pops into your head pops out of your mouth, you might hear yourself remarking, as I once did to a VIP in a hideous necktie: "Any man who could wear a tie like *that* . . ."

Before I could elaborate on the character flaws his choice of neckwear was signaling, he responded: "I never judge a man by his tie. Morty's a good guy. He just dresses like a liberal."

He had mistakenly thought I meant one of his aides, who was wearing a mildly inane pin-dot bow tie.

I was in the midst of relaying this story to my daughter Tina, explaining that the VIP's striped tie clearly marked him as someone who would cynically sell this country down the drain, when I noticed she was not paying attention.

"I might as well talk to myself," I railed at her.

"Oh, weren't you, Mother?" she asked, somewhat surprised.

She is a solitary talker herself. When she was little, she had an imaginary playmate she called Jamie. Jamie, a boy of ultrarefinement, usually joined Tina for tea. These polite exchanges were a pleasure to listen to, but they ended when Tina's sister Bex was born. Though Tina has remained a solitary talker, her subsequent remarks have been lost on me. What did please me, though, was that she thought my comments to her were really meant only for me. It showed that she thought I could still conduct a high level of conversation with myself, and that she was not aware that my solo chats have sunk to mumbles and grunts since I've been living alone.

I see now that just because I am in no danger of being overheard when I talk to myself at home, I must not let my standards slip. I intend to listen carefully for lapses in grammar and to pay close attention to what I say. After all, if the richness of language is to be preserved, it will be saved as much by talking to ourselves as to each other.

The Purse of the Fashion Class

There was no place for pockets in the flimsy, clinging fashions of the Directoire, so the reticule was invented. A silly-looking container, often shaped like an urn, it dangled from long strings and among some was known as "the ridicule." That is not to say it wasn't used for serious purposes: "Madame de B., only you can smuggle the crown jewels out — pray conceal them in your reticule and make haste that they may reach the Vatican by nightfall."

Perhaps the habit of referring to male genitalia as the family jewels started when a man sent on a mission similar to that of Madame de B. stowed the gems in his codpiece, which apart from its decorative function was also used as a cod purse.

"Come, sirrah, have done with rummaging!" one can hear His Holiness snap, clamoring to get his hands on the swag. Small wonder the codpiece was replaced by the drawstring bag, which, without embarrassing preliminaries, could be lightly flung onto the pontiff's lap.

That the handbag has evolved from sources both intimate and ridiculous is no surprise to me.

As a child, I thought of the handbag as an intimate artifact when I was exposed to the voluptuous ones my Jewish aunties carried. The sex appeal of these accessories was short-lived or I might have become a handbag fetishist. The inconvenience of such a fixation can well be imagined ("May I kiss your purse?"), but as it is, I can linger around handbag counters or even take in the "Purses, Pockets, and Pouches" exhibition at the Cooper Hewitt without undue disturbance.

It wasn't so much the sight as the smell of my aunts' bulging purses that was troubling and exciting: a mingling of tobacco, cheap scent (Evening in Paris), Tangee lipstick, chocolate, peppermint, rye bread, herring, pickles, and schmaltz.

"Want a sweet, Figgy?" the aunts would inquire, reaching into their roomy pouches, and I would start guiltily. Sour and sexy, not just sweet, was on my mind as I imagined some barrow boy having his way with me behind the pickle barrel. "Figgy, Figgy," he would pant. Even that nickname — earned when I ate all the figs at a family outing, and used only by the aunts — sounded lascivious with its links to the leaf, to lust, and to original sin. And he would proceed to peel off my clothes as the aunts in their showy way now peeled off the silver paper from the coffee-crème chocolate.

Yet strong as these primal feelings were, I was easily distracted from them (a tendency that *did* become part of my permanent sexual makeup) by the whirling activity generated around the bags as the aunts dipped into them for cut-glass scent bottles with rubber bulbs to spray wrists and throat, for cigarettes from the gilded cases, for polish to paint their nails. All this business not only put my mother's tea — sardines and celery and stale seedcake — in its place, but also brought into focus our dreary suburban life, showing how much more dynamically everyday rituals were performed in the slums of London's East End where the aunts lived.

I wanted to be like my aunts — working in the garment factory, going to the pub and the Palais de Danse, carrying their handbags — until I began to fancy myself as Molly Adaire, foreign correspondent. As I sat in a café in Bucharest opposite William Holden, I would be toying with a glass of wine, not seaside snapshots or my Post Office Savings book — because neither of these items would fit in the slim lizard pocketbook (meant to be seen and not crammed) that was sitting on the table between Bill and me. No, it would be my *life*, not the contents of my handbag, that would be exciting.

Still, even when my aunts' handbags lost their sex appeal, I preferred their world to the stationary one my mother inhabited — a world where nothing more than a change purse was needed for dealings with the greengrocer and butcher. When a visit to the doctor or some special affair called for a handbag, mother got a nondescript pouch from the top of the wardrobe, dusted it off, put a hankie in it, and that was that.

Although she would not have set out to do so (being Anglo-Irish and antimonarchist), Mother was copying royalty. The queen's handbag, then as now, is used as Mother's was: ceremonially. In Mother's case, it was used for status and respectability; in the queen's, rather as an accessory of state in lieu of scepter or orb. Unlike Mother, the queen is never without a handbag; it is on her lap in the dugout canoe on the royal tour, at her feet as she holds the latest grandchild for the royal portrait, beside her breakfast plate as she reads *The Racing Form*. Too bad, then, that it isn't more monarchical: a stately velvet portmanteau with *ER* embroidered in gold thread, or an envelope ablaze with regal insignia suspended from a rope of rubies. Instead, the unrelentingly stodgy style swings from her wrist. No wonder Prince Philip keeps his hand behind his back: if she's ever tempted to say, "Hold my handbag, Philip, while I dub this knight," the royal purse could be swinging from *his* wrist.

One thing the queen does do is keep us aware of the handbag as an *accessory*. The movies used to do that back when the tailored envelope matched the tailored suit and the glamorous jeweled clutch echoed the sparkling evening gown. As a finishing touch, Hollywood handbags were as important as hats, and less limiting — designers didn't have to worry that the oblong pouch made the chin of the leading lady look too large. Like the stars, the bags betrayed no unsightly bulges. The heroine never had to fish for the gun among a muddle of powder puffs, car keys, travel clocks, chewing gum, smelling salts, headache remedies, penknives, toothbrushes, buttons, movie scripts, vitamin pills, pecan rolls, calorie guides, good-luck charms, art erasers, and wallets that were among the items found in the off-duty handbags of Greer Garson, Betty Grable, Claudette Colbert, Lucille Ball, and Maria Montez, as revealed in a 1945 *Life* feature.

Handbag contents still merit magazine scrutiny (wasn't there a piece in *Details* a couple of years ago?), but the only way to get a *true* inventory is by swooping down on the bags unannounced. I'll bet Greer et al. did a little editing before opening theirs up to public inspection. I know I would. It would be out with the stubs of eyeliner, in with the French lipstick in the onyx and diamond case; out with the Chinese-takeout menu, in with the epicurean grocery list (snails, leeks, Madeira, pomegranates); out with the final notices, in with the romantic ultimatums (". . . say you'll be mine or see a world gone mad. If I cannot have you, I shall destroy my media empire. This thing is bigger than both of us. . . . your adoring, Rupert M.").

Why do we have to wait for a magazine exposé to inspire us to carry such diversions in our bags? I'll tell you why. Because we don't switch purses anymore, and we don't pay attention to their contents and possible entertainment value as we once did, back when the handbag completed the fashion statement, the brown calf satchel was unthinkable with the blue suede shoes, and major pocketbook transfers took place daily. Now we may only have twice-a-year turnouts: winter and summer. In my own case, even these semiannual rites aren't particularly thorough — which is why I found flies in my closet last November buzzing around a cotton tote that still contained an evil-smelling T-shirt, a bottle of suntan lotion covered with sand, and a rotting tuna sandwich.

That discovery, witnessed by my daughters, has caused them to call *any* receptacle I carry "the cargo of shame." And given the fact that the handbag not only stirred my earliest and seediest sexual fantasies but today provokes feelings of profound distaste in anyone who superficially examines the contents of my bag, I guess it's a fair description.

Suffering in Style

"So thin! So wan! So wonderful!"

Some assessments of yourself you take more seriously than others. This one, delivered by an old chum, Bronwen, who had arrived from London unaware that my husband had left me, I took to heart.

Everyone else had been saying I was haggard and drawn, scraggy and scrawny. It was time, they said, to put the bloom back in my cheeks, the flesh back on my bones, and to get more nourishment than thin soups and weak tea offered.

But even when Bronwen learned the reason for my condition, she saw no reason to revise her estimate of my appearance.

"A little *tristesse* can work wonders," she said, pressing my hand and calling for champagne as if we had a reason to celebrate. "How lucky your appetite went when he did," she bubbled. "Imagine if you'd flung yourself at the fridge! You'd be in no condition to suffer in style."

Up until then, I hadn't thought of doing much more than

drably moping matters out. "You mean, my husband leaves me and I should look upon it as a fashion opportunity?"

"Precisely. Look at yourself — elevated beyond everyday minor irritations. You're the perfect candidate for tragic chic."

Looking at it in that light, I could see she had a point. Elegiac elegance seemed rather tempting.

"Bronwen, you're amazing," I said gratefully.

"Glad to be of help," she replied, and she went back to London to give others the benefit of her gifts, most notably in her bestseller *The Vogue Body and Beauty Book.*

I've had my lapses since then, but by and large I've tried to make any suffering I do as stylish as possible. And I can pass along a few observations based on what happened to a friend of mine who was deserted by her fiancé and was silly enough to take a therapist's advice about her appearance. "Get into something cheerful," he advised her. And although she had long harbored uneasy thoughts about the therapist's taste in ties and oxblood shoes, she was desperate enough to do as he said.

This is a woman who associates cheerfulness with Santa Claus and seriousness with Saint Laurent, who has often attended to her clothing needs. She was at a loss as to how to go over to the sunny side of the chic.

She decided to start in a small way and soon found herself at the accessory counter, staring at a mirror and appraising her stricken features accessorized with bright red, shaggy earmuffs. A familiar voice suddenly distracted her. Not two counters away, she was startled to discover, stood her ex, with a look of tender indulgence on his face. The look was not meant for her, of course, but for the girl he was with, who was trying on ski goggles.

Earmuffs (unless they are sable) are to ski goggles what vinyl wallets are to Gucci billfolds. Never mind that she had spotted her ex with another woman; the trauma of her fashion gaffe was sufficient to sink my friend into a gloom more profound than any she had experienced since or during the breakup.

Ugly incidents like this can be avoided if we are prepared. As the insurance companies are fond of telling us, disaster can strike at any time, and this is never truer than with the men in our lives.

The end of the love affair finds even the smartest women pitifully equipped to dress for it. I have known some brought so low they are unaware not only that they are wearing the aqua jogging pants with the orange mohair top, but that they have been doing so for a month. Such a boisterous combination might have worked in happier days, but it is not the appropriate outfit for enduring misery with dignity.

The right note to strike is one that is low-key, even somber. Mourning becomes not only Electra but just about everybody. Everything matches, for one thing. There is nothing like basic black from head to toe to signal your state of mind with eloquence. And if you think that is a mite drastic, other sober shades — charcoal, olive, wine — will also give your suffering the setting it deserves.

"What's the difference what I wear?" you may cry out in your anguish. "I'll be suffering in the privacy of my own home."

Even so, you should be ready for house calls. And what if the wandering husband or lover himself stops by? Should you shuffle to the door in the old terry bathrobe he's come to collect? No. You should glide to the door in *another* man's robe. Even if you have to buy it yourself. Splurge on

207

something silky and suave, big enough to swamp you. You will look fragile and fetching, thereby inviting the suspicion that there is a sympathetic sophisticate close by — possibly on the premises — who has been easing your distress.

Misery loves lingerie (his or yours). They've always understood that in the movies. When he asked, "Have you taken leave of your senses?" as he wrestled her for the revolver while she struggled with him in her gorgeous peignoir and nightie, we knew he wasn't including her sense of style.

And remember how Sophia or Liz would always shed the 1950s sheath, all the better to brood in the custom-cut slip? And how many other stars also put on something more comfortable not only to conduct the affair but to mourn its passing?

The tradition is nobly carried on by TV's Alexis and Krystle, who not only do their affluent agonizing in items from the intimate-apparel department, but also in furs, dresses, and panty hose, knockoffs of which are now available in other departments for the loyal fans.

As seductive as grieving in your underwear is, its effect is not to be compared with the striking impact made by the Victorian jiltee, who had to clamber out of crinoline, busks, cages, and other encumbrances before she could languish in dishabille with the sal volatile within her limp reach. When the cad who'd caused her emotions to unravel called to taunt her about her rival, the scheming Lady Meg, he had reckoned without the sight of a modest maiden's untrammeled flesh. Now who's undone! No wonder he sank to his knees, declaring: "You are enchanting in melancholia, Edwina."

Queen Victoria probably thought she was, too. She wore her widow's weeds for fifty years, making it plain that the matter of Albert's passing was far from closed. She couldn't forget him and made sure no one else did either. She knew memories of him might grow dim once she started turning herself out in cerise and lime.

Few people wear mourning now. Even fewer cling to it. Too bad. It's hard enough to sustain heartbreak these days. You're no sooner exposed to it than someone gives you a pill to short-circuit the suffering or rushes you into hypnosis or suggests something to anesthetize the nerve ends. The clothes you're wearing can be an immense help in giving you the chance to experience the mood long enough to bring it to its finest flowering.

Did Edna St. Vincent Millay have the wardrobe? I don't know, but she was good at clinging on. Her sonnet that begins "Time does not bring relief" is the tip-off. In it, she details all the places she can't go to because they recall her lost love — until

> . . . *entering with relief some quiet place*
> *Where never fell his foot or shone his face*
> *I say "There is no memory of him here!"*
> *And so, stand stricken, so remembering him.*

Well, there you are. Clothes are the same as places. You can't stand to wear the Norma Kamali because he adored you in it, and you're also having trouble with the Issey Miyake you bought after the breakup because he *would* have adored you in it.

The only way you can be sure is if you run into him while you have it on. He may, indeed, love your Issey, but that doesn't mean he's going to love you. But he will admire your style.

I frequently encountered my ex while I was suffering in

style and, while none of my outfits reawakened in the man a tender longing for me, I think the air of somber élan — I never wore anything more vibrant than beige — impressed him.

Anyway, I didn't care; I was attracting a different class of man, the sort who'd never given me a nod when I was cheerful and robust. I had cultivated a tremulous air — eyes brimming (not spilling; I didn't want the mascara to run), a catch in the throat, a fluttering of slender hands — and many men found it irresistible. Again and again, I would be pressed to tell my story.

Ultimately, I got rather bored with it, but I was able to write to Bronwen that with such a plethora of eager ears I no longer needed therapy.

"How much more civilized to have a doting man shell out to hear your frets," she wrote, "than to pay a professional to listen."

And, when I think of it, no element of suffering in style was quite as gratifying as that.

Domestic Bliss

There's this plastic ball sitting on my desk. You fill it with detergent and put it in with your wash. There it bobs about, getting clothes cleaner than they otherwise might be. On its side, it says: *"Usare esclusivamente con Dash Liquido."* It will always remind me of how I played house in a Roman palazzo.

Housework is a seductive distraction in New York, where scouring the sink seems infinitely preferable to finishing the magazine article under deadline pressure. Chained to the desk, I yearn to spray and wipe clean, working in rhythm with daytime TV, breaking off every now and then to obey the announcer by dialing the 800 number and ordering some handy household helper ("Send for your ball detergent dispenser today!") guaranteed to give me a sparkling wash instead of the dirty laundry that's been left so long it pulses like a compost heap. Other writers stray to drink or sex. I have to resist the temptation to polish the kettle.

I didn't think I'd be able to indulge in my penchant for

housework at the palazzo. I envisioned myself reduced to wearing pearls at all times and worrying (as Noël Coward, seasoned palazzo visitor, is said to have done) whether the plumbing worked. The palazzo I was going to was built on Roman ruins: wasn't this bound to indicate a fragile and elderly system of pipes?

It was with considerable relief that I arrived and discovered that *palazzo* also means "townhouse," and that the plumbing, late-twentieth-century, was more than a match for any strain I could put on it and, moreover, handled with smooth efficiency the continual loads of laundry it was subjected to by Bronwen.

I should have known not to worry. Let me tell you something about Bronwen, my old friend who has the *appartamento* in the palazzo. She always has impressive addresses — Mayfair, the Hamptons, Klosters, a barge on the Nile — but she never lets that interfere with her fondness for the domestic round. And as a writer herself, she knew she could not give me a better respite from my daily cares than by sticking a dishrag in my hand on arrival.

The basic upkeep of her palazzo is in the hands of Desmond from Bangladesh, who, wise in the ways of deep-down cleanliness, plays Jeeves to Bronwen's Bertie Wooster. While Bronwen attends to the lighter aspects of *lavoro domèstico*, Desmond, having come from a civilization even older than the Roman, knows how to make ancient floors and windows sparkle as they did when Michelangelo slept here.

"Here . . . you mean he slept *here*?" I gasp.

"We like to think so, don't we, Desmond?"

"We do indeed, Madam," Desmond agrees as he polishes

the window of the *salone,* which looks across the narrow, cobblestoned street into the kitchen of the Osteria dell Orso — the hotel where Michelangelo booked a room when he hit town to do the Sistine Chapel. Eventually, he moved into lodgings opposite — and who's to say he didn't settle in Bronwen's actual *appartamento*?

What more thrilling surroundings could I have? I ask myself as I take out Bronwen's garbage. Marveling at how sprightly Italians are, I jump out of the way as a toothless old man, swooping past on his Vespa, lunges at me and my refuse. Then, hearing an outraged scream, I chuckle at the thought of the perky geezer swiftly administering a pinch to the bottom of a less alert pedestrian as he streaks past her. But no, I discover, it is her purse that's been pinched; the hapless victim takes off in helpless pursuit — just like in the American Express ads — leading a posse of Italians all yelling for the *polizia.*

Moments like this make me glad that I'm not out sightseeing but instead doing what travelers to this city have always been told to do. Now that I'm in Rome, I do as the Roman housewife does. Flapping around in carpet slippers, I polish the furniture ("We must guard against waxy buildup," Desmond tactfully cautions); and I treat the Vatican and the Colosseum, the fountains, churches, and statues, as run-of-the-mill neighborhood sights that I may, or may not, notice when I am out on errands buying jasmine plants for Bronwen's terrazzo or Parma ham for lunch.

Of course, I want to get to know Rome — but there will be plenty of time for that when I get back to New York. Like the woman whose baby was admired and said, "Oh, but you should see his picture!" I know I shall really appreciate the place once I start exploring it in books.

Actually, nothing makes me feel more Roman than leaving the city (the natives like nothing more than to get out to the seaside). The train is packed when Bronwen and I take off for the ancient town of Sperlonga, where we'll spend the rest of my holiday.

Here we lodge in the top of an old house with an incredible stairway. Each step is a foot-and-a-half steep, which keeps the elderly ladies who live on the two floors below us quite limber. The climb all but does me in, but I cannot pause on the landings to catch my breath, since I would have to do so under the gaze of these nimble geriatrics, who always sit by their open doors.

The view from the top more than compensates for the agony of getting there. As I hang out the wash, I can take in the mountains, the Mediterranean, and the grotto at the end of the beach where the emperor Tiberius got into various kinds of naughtiness and stashed his statue collection. Over a *caffè* in the Piazza della Republica — a respite earned before tackling the stairs with the groceries — I learn that the statues, or what's left of them, are now in a local museum. They wouldn't be there, I'm told, if the townspeople hadn't turned out to stop the Romans from carting them off when they were unearthed in 1957 during the construction of a coast road.

The description of that event, with the Sperlongese blocking the grotto, hoes and pitchforks in hand, sounds thrilling. Perhaps it's happening again, I think, as later that day cries of "*Chiesa aperto!*" ring in the air, and people all seem to be running in the same direction. Feeling like an extra in a Fellini movie, I leave the onions I am chopping for the pasta, wipe my hands on my apron, and join the crowd making its way through the narrow streets to the twelfth-century church of Saint Rocco, which is being reopened to-day after twenty-seven years because the *belle arti* conser-vationists from Rome want to turn it into a museum. There are mutterings that if it were not for the priest who com-plained about having no place to park his car, the church would never have been closed and desanctified, its beautiful Romanesque interior left to dead cats and dust.

The new church, built beside the parking lot, has all the charm of a multiplex moviehouse. With its sprays of artifi-cial gladioli and wipe-clean plastic statuettes of Jesus Christ and the Virgin Mary, it seems less sanctified than sanitized in its polished-linoleum way.

Perhaps the priest got his low-maintenance house of wor-ship because anything that lightens the load is welcome in a town where many women still do their washing in the stream, beating it white on the stones and using irons that have to be heated over the fire. With this in mind, I'm not surprised that polyester (*uno miracolo!*) is as proudly flaunted as handmade crochet when the bedspreads are hung like banners across the medieval streets for the Corpus Christi parade.

Still, as the little girls in their Communion dresses wind their way through the narrow streets, the Sperlongese do fling real rose petals. The habit ought to be encouraged. "Why settle for confetti?" the ads might ask if San Rocco gets reconsecrated and, perhaps, promoted as *the* spot for nuptials-with-a-difference to be had on the All-Inclusive Wedding and Honeymoon Tour.

Bronwen has already mounted a campaign for recon-secration (although not for the reason mentioned above) and is now scribbling petitions to monsignor friends at the Vatican — which means that I get to do last night's dishes, boil the fish for Dandy the cat, and water the geraniums on the terrazzo. I'm not always this lucky; frankly, there's usually a bit of a scramble for chores. I find myself, in fact, getting resentful that Bronwen always has the best things to do (like cutting up the green beans with her scissors); my mind flashes back to my childhood, when I played house and never got to pour the tea — a deprivation that led to playing doctor instead, a game, I was warned, that could have dark consequences.

Now it looks as if playing house here in Italy might play havoc with my life. I am getting dangerously addicted to it. I find myself trying to iron my bathing suit and continually wearing black to be like the local women (even though my minidress is really an outsize T-shirt).

Where will it all end? I ask myself, as I scrub my cosmetics bag for the fourth time in as many days. Will I get the local sorceress to mix dried blood from my thumb with some local man's expresso, so he will be bewitched into marrying me and keeping me in the drudgery to which I'd like to become accustomed? And as he goes off to milk the buffalo so I can make mozzarella, will I cook and clean from sunup to sundown as I listen to Radio Sperlonga? Radio Sperlonga! That terrible station that plays the same music over and over.

Basta! (*Basta* means "enough," but in this context it means "enough already.") I want to be back where the air is bad, not the airwaves; back where people don't press their jeans and there are dozens of radio stations to play as I polish the food processor.

Food processor! Who am I kidding? The only polishing I do back home is on the word processor. Do I really want to

216

go back to a life where the soothing rhythms of the simple household task are unknown?

It is a bleak prospect. But, as Bronwen says, Italy — with its tiles to be scrubbed, its zucchini to be sliced, its sheets to be ironed — is always waiting for me. And next time, why not have the best of both worlds? Why not jet over with my own laundry, my own sewing?

It is a thought that lightens my heart as I sit at my desk in New York. I could take the saucepans with me and at last reveal the copper bottoms I know to exist under the cooked-on grime! I could take fabric and fashion a slipcover for the couch! I could take the antique meat-grinder, restore it, and test out recipes for homemade Italian sausage!

I am certainly going to take my plastic detergent ball back with me. As I look at it now, it offers a dream of Italy no thought of *pasta con frutta di mare* or the ancient treasures of Rome can provide. And I know my next visit is going to be the vacation of my life.

Gentlemen Callers

When I was a suburban belle, I was never short of gentlemen callers: the butcher with his bloody apron delivering meat wrapped in paper (so much more natural than the plastic-wrapped supermarket trays); the baker with his industrial bread, who nevertheless touched me with his claim "Freshly baked today!" (to which my then-husband unkindly responded, "Surely you mean boiled?"); and even a candlestick (or, at least, a candle) maker, who sold wares from a suitcase that were inclined to explode when lit.

But the milkman was my favorite. Ah, Pierre! There probably wasn't a housewife on his milk route who wasn't at her most ravishing at eight in the morning. Thanks to Pierre, our husbands wished we looked even half as good when they got home from work as when they left for it.

I would try to draw out the daily encounter by ordering extras. "Avez vous le fromage . . . er . . . cottage?" I'd ask, drinking in the sight of him: unmistakably Gallic, despite the uniform, with his beret, his scarf carelessly thrown over one shoulder, a Disque Bleu in the corner of his mouth.

"Kerteedge," he'd repeat. "Mais oui, two percent, n'est-ce pas?" He remembered! My dairy bill was enormous.

"A tout à l'heure!" I'd say, in the happy expectation of seeing him on tomorrow's round, until the dreadful day came when his spectacular sales record earned him promotion to district manager and he was replaced by a likable but not legendary man called Bud.

Since I moved to Manhattan, regular gentleman callers have been whittled down to a minimum. The teenage boy from the Chinese takeout comes frequently and always says, "How are we tonight?" – but this is not a sign of a growing relationship so much as a confirmation of me as repeat customer, because although the greeting is always the same, he isn't.

The Con Ed man might be lovely Peter, meter man, but how can I tell? He has never said anything more illuminating to me in our brief encounters than "Have a nice day."

No such meaningless benediction would ever pass the lips of my West Indian exterminator, a gentleman and a martyr who sacrificed himself inhaling poisonous fumes so that I might be rid of roaches and, having succeeded, no longer blesses my house with his saintly presence.

Still, be they benign or not, I do not care for extended calls. Not even house calls by the doctor. Ever since Camille, being sick is no excuse not to look your best; and even when house calls were still being made, I was never one who could manage to bloom in illness and lie abed attractively flushed with fever, in freshly laundered flannelette.

Now it is the hairdresser who makes house calls, and once again I am found wanting. When Mr. Terry called on me, he disdained my suggestion that he make himself at home, and instead perched fastidiously on the edge of a chair while I went off to shampoo my hair in the shower, something I should have done before he arrived. He expressed his irritation about that, but didn't mind that not a single mirror in the house was positioned to provide him with the right light.

"A sculptor doesn't work in front of a mirror and I don't require one either," he said, as he sat me near the window and fastened a plastic capelet over the T-shirt I wear when I dye my hair.

"No, quite," I agreed cravenly, instead of protesting that a sculptor works with dead substances, not with hair attached to a living human being, and that I had a right to see what was being done to me.

When I finally got the chance to examine it, I saw that the cut — brilliant, elegant, refined — served only to heighten the deficiencies of the face it framed. "Why don't you take it with you and give it to someone it will suit," I should have said in a lighthearted tone that would mask my misery. But I wasn't up to it. Wretched in my T-shirt spotted with henna and other hair shades, I was reduced in much the same way as when the doctor called on me and I could see he was thinking it was squalor such as mine that *created* flu viruses, as I lay in my sickbed in a sleazy nightie and pilled cardigan.

Being put in your place when you are already in it is not an attractive experience. And that is why throwing just anything on to receive gentlemen with insurance to sell, or samples, tape measures, and easy payment plans to fuss over, is not a good idea. These callers will get the better of you unless you're dressed to prevent it. In my own case, my confidence quotient is vastly increased if I simply remember to put on a skirt or pants with pockets in the side seams. With my helplessly fluttering hands out of sight, the likelihood of my being talked into the aqua paisley is considerably reduced (though not eliminated entirely, alas) and I may even demand to have clause 3B of the policy explained again.

For the lightning visit (Con Ed, say), the bathrobe will do. Not, however, the bath towel. That is all an English friend of mine with an arrogant disregard for the laboring classes was wearing when a man came to fix the air conditioner. After leering at her and taking twice as long as necessary to do the job, he finally left. "What on earth was wrong with him?" she asked. Had I not been there, she might have found out.

As far as I am concerned, you should never be wearing anything even faintly provocative when a serviceman calls. Indeed, I have often felt that the sight of my dirty underwear in the laundry basket would be all that would be needed to drive the washing-machine man mad with lust. Perhaps he wouldn't even need that provocation. He might think himself justified in visiting his lowest urges on me as a fit punishment for a harlot whose baleful presence had bewitched the machine and caused the breakdown, much as menstruating women were once thought to turn milk sour.

I no longer worry about being attacked for casting evil spells on major appliances, but that's because I no longer have any big enough to rate service calls. In fact, I rarely summon men to render services of any sort, although my friends tell me that if there were ever a time to have shelves built, walls painted, and floors stripped and lacquered, it is now, when so many gentlemen with glamorous credentials — poets, painters, filmmakers, moguls-in-the-making, PhD's — are doing it.

With the appearance of these gentlemen, my friends claim, the golden age of gentlemen calling has arrived. But in my experience, even though such pedigreed callers may bring passing enlightenment, to look to them for romance or even a job well done is to doom yourself to disappointment.

The MBA who is chinning himself in your kitchen doorway today could very well be heading the largest chain of health spas in history tomorrow, but in the meantime, he'll do a rotten job of cleaning your oven; the filmmaker who is brilliantly dissecting (and demolishing) the Spielberg school cannot do that and professionally paint your bathroom at the same time.

You may have signaled your willingness to allow these callers to do their chin-ups, write their screenplays, and otherwise advance their outside careers while on your payroll if having initially appeared with your hair barely combed you were never seen by them thereafter without eye makeup. Do not break the never-look-alluring-for-the-handyman rule. Even if he has a college degree.

He may continue to improve in your eyes, but despite your most strenuous efforts, you will likely remain the same in his. To him, you are a person in a settled if not stagnant situation — apartment bought, belongings insured, three locks on your door. Cry in vain that such attainments are only stepping-stones on your own upward path; to him, they are the end of the line. In his estimation, you have gone about as far as you can go. You are all but entombed. He, on the other hand, is a free spirit for whom destiny waits and the future lies ahead.

When Hollywood beckons, he will remember you — if at all — for the grit embedded in the windowsill he never finished painting. And even if he grows tired of waiting for Donald Trump to finance his spas and decides to let himself go to pot and move in with you, you will still date the deterioration of your life from the time he first called and was meant to defrost the fridge but went jogging instead.

Gentlemen callers do not exist to provide us with a future but with a mythic presence. That is why, ideally, they should be encountered fleetingly on the threshold of your world. Let such a caller conjecture that the life that lies beyond the door is as inviting as the woman who is framed by it. Never ask him in to find out.

There is a shortage of such callers in Manhattan, but that could be remedied if street vendors were transformed to peddlers and licensed to call.

This could be a happy move all around. Stationed on the sidewalks, vendors are an affront to shopkeepers, who resent their lack of overhead and their pricing structure, which they claim are possible only when goods cost nothing in the first place.

Despite the advantages the vendor enjoys over Bloomingdale's, he is often hard put to scratch out a living and would undoubtedly jump at the chance to improve his lot by pulling up his mat of trinkets and taking it door-to-door.

Once he no longer enlivened the sidewalk, he would be a perambulating delight to the lady of the house, who would never know whether the next gentleman examined through the peephole would be offering an armful of handbags or a stack of old magazines.

And then, why not license beggars, too?

As matters stand, unwilling to stop and fumble for change or indignant at being accosted on our busy rounds, we brush past the outstretched hand. Later, on the nightly news, the plight of the mendicant (as William F. Buckley likes to call him) is brought alive to us in a way that it never is on the street. If at that moment the doorbell should ring, offering us the opportunity to play lady bountiful to a gentleman in distress, would we be likely to pass it up? Perhaps. But at any rate, the beggar still will have improved his lot, even if only slightly: as he petitions apartment buildings door-to-door, at least he has a roof over his head.

When you think of it, beggars and peddlers were almost certainly the world's first gentlemen callers. What better group, then, to license and thus keep this time-honored ritual alive?

A Dyeing Art

Before moving to my New York apartment, I'd have dyeing jags. Usually I'd be seized by a fit to change something from insipid to dynamic by seven o'clock. But whether I was acting on impulse or had time to plot a color change, I was consistently slapdash, never taking any more trouble with the actual dyeing beyond throwing the article into the washing machine along with several packets of dye. Perhaps if I had been careful, the results would have been more lasting. As it was, I got once-in-a-lifetime colors that were gone with the next wash. But who needed colorfastness? After all, in memory, the blue that faded was as ravishing as any created.

Not everything could be dyed, I discovered. I often got hideously patchy results when something I'd thought was pure cotton contained traces of undyeable polyester or acrylic. I was never deterred by such failures, especially in the years when I was part domestic drudge and part poorly paid broadcaster and writer; if it hadn't been for dyeing, I would have had no dazzle at all.

"What an astonishing moss!" Cecil Beaton said as we faced each other over the mike and I suddenly knew that I was on a wavelength with him that I could never have achieved with the original boring beige of my commonplace shirt.

I would never have discovered the delights of dyeing if it hadn't been for Avril. Until I met her, I had a notion the process involved boiling vats, testing temperatures, opening windows, locking up cats — endless trouble to get a color that, far from reviving some old dress, would only make it look worse. The first time I saw Avril, she was wearing a dirndl skirt in a totally personal purple. I was floored. How could this garment — which looked, frankly, as if it had been taken from the basement rack — boast a color of such startling originality and uniqueness?

The answer wasn't long in forthcoming. Avril always had dyeing to do, and she invited me to witness the transformation of tablecloth and napkins from off-white to copper. It didn't take but a few minutes, once the washing machine filled, for her to shake in a packet of this and that, then add a couple of dish towels when the dye got too dense. For the rest of the time, we drank coffee and talked about how I need never again be defeated by the crass colors of modern life.

That very day, it was into *my* washing machine with an Indian bedspread, which emerged with its dirty cream background a shimmering emerald. True, the design was somewhat obscured, but I happily trilled, "You can't have everything" — a phrase I was to repeat through dozens of dyeings.

Those first few weeks of color control went to my head — and to my hands, which were stained from all the times I stopped the machine to fish around and see if the pot holder was taking the dye as well as the bath mat and the

T-shirt. The thing was, I never had a clear idea of what I'd end up with. I'd start out vaguely in the direction of old gold and find myself landed with an unpleasantly murky mustard.

These disasters pleased my husband no end. A frequent victim of my careless dyeing habits — more than once, an unrinsed machine would turn a shirt of his from brand-new white to secondhand rose — he sided with my mother in denouncing the whole business. Mother, in her obsessive quest for cleanliness, believed in bleaching out color, never mind putting it in. She warned that my mania for dyeing was not only a serious threat to my marriage but could well unbalance my daughter.

"A baby in black!" she said, deeply shocked. "It's against nature."

I didn't think so. On the contrary, I thought black far more flattering on white babies than wishy-washy pastels. Other babies paled beside mine, intense in her black (once buttercup or pale blue) rompers and smocks. I looked upon this aspect of my dyeing as the most innovative I had ever done, and I dreamed of it attracting the attention of some fashion editor, who would display me and my baby in a black-and-white center spread.

Nothing like that happened; mother took the baby out on a hot day and noticed the dye rubbing off on my daughter's neck and wrists. Appalled, she washed all the rompers and smocks until she'd reduced them to a shade my husband called gulag gray. I felt bitterly disappointed at this setback. Impressing Cecil Beaton was one thing, but I craved admiration closer to home.

An opportunity seemed to present itself when I was sent to do a story on an organic dyer. It wasn't my first exposure to such a person. When I was growing up, we had a neighbor, old Mrs. Groots, who wore streaky tan gloves that she'd dyed by dipping them in tea.

But the organic dyer I was assigned to profile sounded more promising. It was said she'd boiled up bark, berries, flowers, vegetables, and fruit in rainwater and dyed dog's hair with the results. I imagined her as a sort of Merry Meg of the Moors — togged out in elderberry wools and spinach linens; hair, dipped in the beet pot, a flaming ruby and tied back with dried grass; a dog dyed goldenrod, yapping at her heels. Perhaps she would have a frog or two in her pockets.

I hoped to find out from her how to extract the shimmering promise from onion skins, and I saw myself, armed with this knowledge, dyeing a cobwebby sort of dress palest gold and appearing in it — a lily of the field that Saint Laurent in all his glory could not . . . and so on.

But the organic dyer was polyester from head to toe and as conventional as a shopping mall. Her quirky output — all that hand-spinning (it was hair *of*, not *on*, the dog), hand-dyeing, and hand-looming — didn't end up on her back but on the wall, in hangings more impressive for how they were done than for how they looked. I thought the colors distinctly tepid.

She was more than willing to slip me a few tips, but it all seemed like a lot of bother to someone like me who dyed, after all, for no-fuss instant results. Besides, you didn't just boil up the apple bark, you had to use chemicals: potassium dichromate, stannous chloride, ferrous sulfate, and poisonous mordants. *Not* the stuff to have around a husband of uncertain temper.

Anyway, dyeing was *real* life to me. Not some out-of-this-world, weirdo pursuit, but an inextricable part of my domestic routine like cooking and cleaning. Sometimes it even *replaced* cleaning: impatient for results, I often dyed things instead of washing them.

There were times, however, when I dyed more than others. When my husband and I split up, my dyeing output fell, confirming my mother's suspicions that I'd done it all along to drive him away. The true reason was simpler: a lot of my dyeing had to do with entertaining for him, and when he went, so did the need for a cerise tablecloth.

Just the same, my weekly shopping list still included packets of dye, which I had always bought like other women buy washday products, and flurries of coloring came and went. Many of my friends still believed I was doing too much of it. Dyeing was tying me to the washing machine, they said; I ought to be out and about in the pink, not hanging around the house waiting for it to turn scarlet.

One lover urged me to take stock of my life — did I want to be a colorist or a novelist? What they all failed to realize was that I wasn't into dyeing for the sake of the vivid colors so much as to find a way to render myself unique.

The fact that I chose this particular method could well go back to my mother's forebears (though the family proclivity skipped a generation, in her case), to those ancient Britons who dyed their bodies blue and, apart from giving themselves a unique identity, felt that if stripped by their enemies, they'd still have something on.

The drive to be distinctive with color, I was reading in the *New York Times*, goes back to the Iron Age. It was once thought that royal purple, which was produced so kings and high priests wouldn't have to look like everyone else, started with the Phoenicians, but now archeochemists have discovered much earlier origins.

It was such a laborious process to get this dye that it was as precious as gold. First, you had to harvest millions of whelks, those mollusks that are a bit like snails; then you had to take out the meat, which had the gland in it that emitted the dye rather like a squid squirts ink.

Can't you see those ancient dye-makers, sitting on some Mediterranean beach in their dun-colored tatters, with shells piling around them as they dug out whelk flesh and chucked it into pits to putrefy before boiling it up for days in special vats? It took eight thousand pounds of whelk flesh to produce five hundred pounds of dyestuff, but the colors — blue, to violet, to black purple — made it all worthwhile. Pliny the Elder thought the most desirable shade was that of congealed blood; but as a mere writer and commander of the fleet, would he have been allowed to wear it? Sumptuary laws don't dictate color use now — money does. As a rule, the cheaper the cloth, the more vulgar the color; but even in expensive fabrics, it is disconcerting to see how abysmally ordinary colors often are.

"Seven hundred dollars!" I once heard a woman exclaim over a taffeta ballgown. "That aqua belongs on a beach ball."

It did.

In my price range, the dominance of royal blue and red causes me to retreat to black, gray, brown, and beige, yearning for the days when I had a machine and could dye at will. At one point, the sense of deprivation was keen enough to drive me to hand-dyeing in the sink. I changed a terry robe from white to chocolate and switched a chemical-warfare jacket from military green to an interesting moldy black; but when I failed to restore a balloon suit I'd got on sale at Charivari to its former vigor (the faded parts stubbornly remained lighter than the rest), I gave up.

I'm told a VCR would bring me a richer life, but I believe I can live without one. What I need is something more fundamental: an apartment-sized washing machine, and maybe a small spin dryer. In other words, the means to lift my belongings from the drab or, if they are too exuberant, put them into it.

The Staff of Lifestyle

"Let them eat bread," Gorbachev could well have said in encouraging the export of Russia's dark rye to the United States, where it will sell for $4.15 a loaf.

Of course, Les Fashionábles will not actually *eat* it — but it will be indispensable at dinner parties. "The centerpiece for our gala on the fifth — Minnie and Mickey Mouse as Bolshoi Ballet dancers carved out of authentic Russian rye — was designed by Jeff Koons," Ivana Trump will say, "but the actual *cutting* of the loaf will be done in Italy."

I have to admit bread brings out the faddist in me, particularly when it is part of a bigger philosophical movement; and surely nothing could be more significant of Russia's move toward capitalism than the transformation of worker's bread into a gourmet item.

It could well be the most important thing that has happened to bread since the sixties, when those of us with a need to be socially significant *and* trendy satisfied it by baking our own.

"Bake your own bread?" my husband sneered. "You can't be bothered to slice it."

That wasn't altogether true. I simply bent to pressure from the children, who preferred the precut loaf — although I resisted their pleas for white and insisted on the kind dyed to resemble whole wheat. Waving a slice of it at my husband, I said: "I don't even believe this is made from flour. It's just layers of chemical gauze compressed together to form slices and then injected with synthetic breadlike flavor."

"And vitamins," he said.

"Only because the same people who bring us nuclear arms and toxic waste have taken them out in the first place."

"It's all the same group?" he asked — he was always politically naive.

"More or less." I wasn't sure, but it seemed logical. "Why wouldn't they control bread? It's so basic."

I wouldn't have bothered to convince him except that I wanted him to see that baking bread was going to bring far reaching changes in our lives: once you start baking bread, you start soaking beans (you don't just open a can); you start judging a fish in the flesh (not by his picture on the frozen food box); you start preserving fruit (not buying it ready-prepared in the jar of jam).

As it turned out, I never got around to all the other stuff. Baking took up a great deal of my time — but my children will never forget the bread I made: "It tastes homemade," they will say to this day if ever they want to describe a substandard bakery product.

Actually, it wasn't so much the taste as the texture. Since they were used to the stuff that melts in your mouth, they found my bread intolerably dense and heavy. I thought it rather biblical, and possibly what the staff of life, in its semi-leavened state, was meant to be.

I did attempt to get an airier texture, but the only time I could get the dough to rise was when it got lodged under my wedding ring. If it responded only to body heat, what was I to do, strap it to my stomach? Obviously not. I put it on top of the radiator, hoping this location would induce it to double in size. When it failed to do so, I lost patience, and it was into the oven, ready or not.

It was often soggy in the middle.

I could probably have baked bread as well as the next person if I had used commercial, no-fail ingredients, but I got mine from the health food store. The man who ran it, I see now, was brazenly out to make a killing off the counter-culture and was just as unscrupulous, in his small way, as the military-industrial complex. His prices were outrageous; his quality, questionable. I once bought a bag of flour from him and later found weevils in it. When my daughter, without telling me, took the infested grain to school for show-and-tell, I got an embarrassing call from the Health Department. Who's to say his inferior merchandise wasn't the problem?

Even if it wasn't, as a fast-paced, urban person, I was getting restless with the slow-moving world of organic-bread baking, and when offered the chance to work as a fashion publicist, I took it. After all, fashion had its share of rebels too, and no doubt I could continue my role as activist at a pace more suited to my temperament.

"I'm afraid you're not going to have Mommy home all the time, anymore," I said to my daughters.

"Does that mean we can have bread from the store?" they asked.

Propelled by their ungrateful attitude, I went off with less trepidation than most mothers might have — to Prague, where we were to shoot promotional photographs of a collection by a Czech-born designer who had fled to the West some years earlier, and who now hoped the drabness of her birthplace would make her styles look rather smarter by contrast than they actually were.

By stressing to the Czechs that it was historical settings we were interested in, we had their full cooperation, including the use of two local models who were the only heavy bread eaters I have ever come across in their profession. Every morning these girls would arrive with half a loaf and a hunk of sausage as their breakfast. And while they weren't as wispy as Western models, they nevertheless were slim, so I could only presume that the rest of the time they lived on watery soup made from vegetable roots and had been issued bread and sausage merely to impress us capitalists.

I suppose it is because I had come so recently from baking my own bread, but the models' breakfast is my abiding memory of that trip. No wonder I thought of Ivana Trump (originally Czech) when I envisioned imported Russian rye playing a leading role in New York society. And goodness knows what it will be tomorrow. The Russians boast they have one hundred different types of bread; it sells over there for about twenty cents a loaf — a markup of more than two thousand percent for America! As far as I am concerned, all that bread is a good enough reason to stay away from the place. It wouldn't take me long to look as bulky as a Muscovite in midwinter.

I have a weakness for bread and cannot trust myself around it — as I demonstrated when taken to tea at the Carlyle by a Canadian editor. The purpose of our meeting was to discuss the subject of some articles I might do, not the terms under which they would be undertaken. But when I fell on the delicate little sandwiches that were served, the editor looked alarmed and offered me an advance. If I'd nibbled on the sole Bercy when we lunched together, I would have been deprived of cash up front.

It's nice to think my weakness for bread can have such happy results. Usually, I have to observe extreme caution in my daily intake. When dining out, I must find the strength to wave away the basket. I dare not keep bread in the house, and the casual invitation to grab a sandwich is not for me. Alas, it is not just the tiny tea sandwich that seduces me but the towering club: while others may dream of eating lobster ragout with Julia Child, I think of joining Dagwood Bumstead, deliriously piling filling on slice, filling on slice, and cementing this edifice of turkey, bacon, tuna, egg, tomato, and lettuce with mayo, mayo, mayo.

On hearing this, people say you must love the submarine. Well, no, I don't. For me, the ideal approach to the long loaf, at least the baguette, if you want it to function as a sandwich, is the one taken by M. F. K. Fisher. She suggests splitting the baguette, spreading it with sweet butter mixed with Dijon mustard, tenderly laying thin slices of ham on the bottom half, wrapping it in paper and a towel, and sitting on it. The amount of time you do so depends on your body weight. If you weigh 110 pounds, you'll need to sit for about twenty minutes. If you're heavier, it doesn't take as long. I brooded over the newspaper while I did it (you work out how much

I weigh) and then took it along on a picnic with my daughters.

"This is great, Mom," they said. I am ashamed to say I did not give M. F. K. the credit. Instead, I said, "Remember when I had this theory about body heat and bread? Well, I thought, what if I sat on a baguette . . . ?"

If you're thinking of doing it, let me warn you the results will be disappointing if you plan on using one of those phony "French" loaves of white aerated sponge with a "crust" that is just as likely to shatter into powder as crumbs. And for many Americans, that is all that is available. This country was built on quick breads — from the corn pone of the settlers to the stuff they force into fast rising in the factories. Though the Russians might be behind in everything else, they are ahead of us in bread. But if the dissidents and defectors are disappointed with our version of it (as Solzhenitsyn is with our godlessness), I have never heard them mention it in their list of complaints.

In fact, if you go out to the Russian restaurants in Brighton Beach, Brooklyn, you will find assembly-line rye piled high among the herring and sour cream and shashlik and stuffed cabbage and bowls of borscht and bottles of soft drinks. Everyone stuffs it down and smokes, and, in between bites and puffs, dances to tunes like "As Time Goes By." It is like being whisked back to the forties, to an America that no longer exists.

Perhaps the Russia of the deep, dark rye that has sustained it through czar, revolution, commissars, massacres, and wars doesn't exist either, and is for export only to decorate the dinner tables of socialites.

Perhaps, with *perestroika*, traditional Russian bread will

not only seem heavy and old-fashioned but be deemed an impediment to progress; if it's going to get moving, Russia will need the new lite bread of the West.

Someone once said we had nothing to fear from the Russians, since they didn't even know how to make a good toaster. We *do* know how to make a good toaster — an expertise born, as much as anything else, in order to make our bread palatable. But what if the Russians get better at making toasters than bread? What then?

My own view is that the CIA should spread the word that Amerikansky bread ruins the bowels, and that Russians should stick with their ancient bread-baking ways for the sake of the nation's health. Then they won't have time to muck about with toasters, which can only lead to a Soviet buildup of major appliances; we've had enough of that to put up with from Japan.

Don't beat around the Bush, George, send the message loud and clear: "Let *them* eat bread!"

Making a Scene

Years ago, when I worked in a solicitor's office in London, a gentle old clerk who'd been with the firm for forty-eight years was retired. The presentation of a watch to the old man, it was decided, would take place on our tea break so it wouldn't interrupt the flow of work.

"Let's hope he doesn't make a scene and break down," the senior partner said before the ceremony.

He didn't. I did. The lump in my throat developed into tears and then sobs I could not control. Everyone was embarrassed, including the old chap, who later not only confided to the mailroom boy that he thought I had spoiled his big moment, but asked if I had foreign blood. I was fired a week later.

It was apparent, I was told on being dismissed, that I had very little rein on my emotions if I could get so worked up over something that didn't really concern me. How I'd carry on if directly affected — there had already been an ugly eruption over a request to retype a brief that bore a sardine stain — was too awful to contemplate. Displays of temperament, I should remember, had no place in the business world.

I certainly didn't agree with that. I felt they were the only things that made office life tolerable, and I went on creating them and losing jobs for years. Life in the typing pool would have been drab indeed without those flamboyant little exercises staged at the typewriter or in the Ladies', where I usually fled to sob if I felt myself slighted.

The women I worked with were for the most part quick to denounce my episodes and disassociate themselves from me, especially those of iron resolve who were convinced that the ticket to the top was icy calm. Not that it did them any good. Although I was trotted out as Exhibit A when the men fell to discussing the unsuitability of women for the business world, the other women were also included, with their self-control dismissed as a sign of unhealthy repression.

They might just as well have let rip. It might have done some good by providing a release from tension and tedium. Apart from that, who is to say that making a scene — particularly if it's an occasional and brief one — cannot be a useful career tool? The threat of it coming from the right quarter should never be underestimated.

Not that I ever staged scenes for profit. I was simply raised to do it. My family *communicated* that way. We lived at a pitch I thought commonplace (and it might have been if I'd been raised in an ebullient New York neighborhood and not a stolid London one); normal conversation was conducted in raised voices and a brisk exchange of hostilities marked mealtimes.

School was difficult because control was stressed. Since I'd never been taught to repress outbursts, the mildest rebuke would either incite an inflammatory response or produce floods of tears. I was known as a hothead and a blubberer — not an attractive combination. I might have had a more dignified reputation if I could have exercised my temperament in classroom discussion, but my temperament was the very reason I was excluded. ("Freda, you are shouting and being unpleasant again. Do sit down and be quiet.") Usually the subject under discussion was as tame as a muffin for someone like me, who yearned to discuss politics and religion — two subjects we girls were warned to avoid on the grounds they could provoke nastiness in even the most reasonably minded person.

Naturally, I burned to engage in these forbidden topics outside the classroom. The thought of tackling the retired missionary couple who lived next door with the fact that the conversion of the heathen was just another cheap imperialist ploy was powerfully seductive.

One day, unable to resist the temptation any longer, I yelled at the wife as she hung out her wash, "Keep Christ out of Kenya!" But she was hard-of-hearing and only smiled and said, "It will be all right, dear, if the rain holds off."

She may have been trying to avoid a scene, a common enough occupation in our neighborhood, where those who sustained a crisis — loss of job, spouse, faculties, hope — without kicking up a fuss were to be admired.

"She made a proper fool of herself," neighbors reported on returning from a funeral at which one of their number had tried to fling herself into her husband's grave.

I found such dramatic behavior entrancing whether encountered in real life or at the movies — where, as far as I

241

was concerned, those who made the scenes stole them. I always felt a particular sympathy for the heiress, who was invariably in the wrong clothes when disaster struck. Looking silly in sequins, she would find her screams cut off by the heroine — a spunky girl of modest means, stunningly appropriate in jodhpurs, boots, and open-necked shirt — who'd slap her and snap: "Daddy isn't going to buy you out of this one, Ursula."

The habitual scene maker is rarely dressed properly for the eruption. Too often I've lost my case by wearing something, like a nightie, that could be taken down and used against me by an adversary who employed seduction to make me forget my grievances. Worse, when at four in the morning he was long past either love or war, I would find myself unwilling to waste the nightie, reduced not only to railing, but also to flaunting myself at him.

If I couldn't score points with *my* clothing, I could certainly do it with his. God knows where I got the strength, but I tore my ex-husband's raincoat in two when I found out he'd bought his mistress lumber for bookshelves. Besides being enraged that he was going to build them for her ("Pass the hammer, sweetheart"), I didn't want to think of her *having* books.

I nursed the illusion for years that the scenes I staged were unique. I have since learned that the rending of raincoats is by no means rare, and have moved to New York, where I regularly witness similar tiffs on the corner of my street. The buildings surrounding my apartment create acoustical conditions that might be the envy of Carnegie Hall. Even on the seventh floor, I can catch the querulous outrage in "Don't you turn your back on me!" and similar expressions with an all-too-familiar ring.

Finally, rather than be reminded of the lamentable standard of my own confrontations, I stopped watching. Not that I was deprived. Living in New York, you need never lack for drama, and an excellent spot for taking in such diversions is my local supermarket at Ninety-second and Broadway. I cherish the memory of the boy who pushed his cart into the heels of an elderly woman who was shopping there.

"Watch yo ass, lady," he advised her.

Turning to face him, she said: "I cain't, honey, cos I ain't like you. I ain't no mutant. I ain't got no eyes in the back of my head."

It is courageous to cause a scene in New York, where the mildest protest is likely to provoke a violent reaction. (I worried for days that the bully was merely waiting for his chance to take revenge on the old lady for making him a laughingstock.) But even if it weren't risky, New Yorkers don't have time for scenes or those who make them. That is why it is usually out-of-towners who, in the mistaken belief that their fellow passengers will support them, deliver a lecture on politeness to the subway clerk, only to find that when he rudely dismisses them with "Stand aside!" the cry is taken up by those on line.

I have often been tempted to give a piece of my mind to those messianic maniacs who ask us to pause in the headlong subway rush to reflect on the possibility of eternal damnation. But I know I would regret this step; because if there is one thing these evangelists crave, it is to be challenged ("Revile me, spit on me!"), and I would invite their attentions all the way to my stop, if not to the hereafter.

In my experience, a satisfactory scene cannot be had with someone who is eager for it. Having a scene should not be a collaborative process with each person speaking in turn and repeating what the other has said to make sure it's been heard right.

"You are a motherfucking son of a bitch."

"Are you calling me a motherfucking son of a bitch, you motherfucking son of a bitch?"

"You're fucking right, you motherfucking son of a bitch."

"Nobody calls me a motherfucking son of a bitch."

"Well *I'm* calling you . . ."

This exchange will go on endlessly, with neither antagonist quite willing to trust the evidence of his ears or give eavesdroppers (or even the adversary) an account of the details behind the argument.

Well, when I stage public demonstrations, I happily spell out my grievances. I remember glowering across the room once as my ex flirted with a restaurant critic; the sound of her announcement that he was going to be her taster when she reviewed a new Thai restaurant brought me swiftly to her side.

"Make sure the creep has a doggie bag for the children and me," I urged her in a voice that carried to every corner of the room. "Our food budget hasn't stretched beyond chicken wings for a month."

Such outbursts did not succeed in keeping my husband from his assignations. If it wasn't a restaurant critic, it was an image maker, a ballet dancer, or a Realtor — all chosen, as much as anything else, for their aversion to public scenes.

When my husband found me cool as any restaurant critic when we met to discuss the details of our divorce, he nervously confessed that he had expected me to throw a fit before the lunch was over.

But I put his fears to rest: "Why should I," I demanded to know, "now that I no longer care?"

Forgetting the dozens and dozens of explosive moments between us, the sight of me coolly raising my spoon from my crab bisque was more than he could bear. He was suddenly overcome with emotion. His eyes filled with tears; he fumbled for my hand, knocked over a glass of wine, and said brokenly: "Darling . . ."

"Please," I hissed. "Let's not have a scene."

Nights Out

Deprived of the glamour and excitement of nightlife, I've always found comfort in thinking that although early to bed, early to rise might not make us healthy, wealthy, and wise, our prospects are at least better than if we stay out all night — a habit that can only lead to ruin.

Now the startling possibility has arisen that only losers are in bed by eleven. It is those who are burning the candle at both ends who can expect to live life to the fullest.

This unwelcome news appeared in the April 1989 issue of *Glamour* via a group of people deeply committed (as door-persons, emcees, club owners, and whatnot) to New York's downtown club scene, which rarely gets underway before midnight. Despite (or because) of the hours they keep, they are, they claim, not only more active and ambitious than the rest of us but *healthier*, having disavowed drink, drugs, red meat, and the false restrictions of regular hours, in favor of vitamins, vegetarian diets, and the observation of their natural time clocks.

Their days, they say, are as healthful as their nights. I see them starting with the dawn swim at the pool, followed by the vigorous bout of calisthenics and the ten-minute yoga trance to focus energy for the power lunch, after which it's the salon appointment, where the hair is dimensionally dyed (blond, blonder, blondest) while they nap under a yogurt-and-cucumber mask, which is just the revitalizer needed for cocktails (nothing stronger than Evian water) with the literary crowd at the Royalton; then it's home for a good night's sleep — 8 to 10 PM — while learning Greek via subliminal lessons on audiocassette. On awakening, it's off to the clubs for another exciting night of mental stimulation and aerobic exertion (what is dancing, after all?).

I cannot pretend to be ignorant of the possibility that there is more to be gained from staying out all night than slaving away all day, because in 1977, as a columnist for the *Montreal Star*, I was invited to New York to attend a party at Regine's.

According to a mimeographed list handed me at the door, Andy Warhol, Mick Jagger, and the Duke and Duchess of Marlborough were expected. The one person who wasn't going to be there was Regine. That was a blow. Imagine going to Rick's Café in Casablanca and finding it was Humphrey Bogart's night off?

Still, there was the chance that Andy Warhol would ask me to pose for his Polaroid and, on examining the results, announce: "I'd like to take a few dozen more of these and make you a famous Factory product."

But neither Andy nor the Marlboroughs nor Mick showed up, and it was the publicity person who wanted my picture and suggested it be taken with Shelley Hack. This was a dismal prospect. I saw myself selected, like the peasant on the fashion shoot, only for the shorter, stouter, more brutal contrast I would provide to Her Hackness. But after the photo was taken, I began to think I might not have looked too bad, because the flash of the strobe brought a man to my side who inquired: "Are *you* anyone?"

"Well, I'm not just another Hack," I said, thinking to make light of the odious comparison he was bound to have made, and also to assure him that I was a cut above the usual reporter.

I must have made some impression, because he seemed eager for me to know that he was a designer ("My card"). Whatever success attended his daylight hours was nothing compared to his nightlife. It was here, he said, that stars were born, contacts made, deals arranged, romances launched. The ceaseless round was made possible by his patronage of revivifying gyms (more cards), as well as regular trips to European spas (more cards yet) for a complete overhaul.

Even a PR man, which is what he turned out to be, can come up with the odd revelation. His schedule left me distinctly unsettled. What, I asked myself, was I doing with my life but letting my mind and muscles atrophy in useless sleep? My idea of nightlife — loosely based on the consumptive, opium-dosed, and decadent Berlin cabarets of the thirties — was obviously passé.

No longer could I thank my lucky stars that I didn't have to bother with the clubs, that I could lead a full, rich life by settling smugly into bed with my cocoa and my book. Now such behavior seemed merely sluggish. As I pulled back the covers, an unsettling voice would whisper into my ear: "The night has just begun." This was no time to be climbing into my flannelette nightie.

Shortly afterward, I moved to Manhattan and brought

this dismaying revelation with me. My work as a broadcaster and reporter gave me ample opportunity to sample the clubs: MK, Tunnel, Bolido's, Peggy Sue's, Palladium, Area, Red Zone, Limelight. Remember those names, because they will probably all have disappeared by the time you read this. Still, my exposure to them cannot be said to have improved my life — largely, I suppose, because I was always in them during off-hours, having been invited to draw the attention of the public to this film, that book, or the Boy George concert tour.

But if I failed to improve my own life, I did no end of good for my daughter Sophie's by maintaining the fiction that I went to the clubs as a regular and thereby impressing her teenage friends. Other mothers might be on a first-name basis with Mario Cuomo; *I* was recognized by the doorman at Tunnel (I must be — how else would I get in?). Although I was no more part of the scene than the office cleaner is part of the corporate world, my detailed descriptions of the bathroom at Nell's had the kids fooled.

There were times when I thought I had it all — in reality I was lying in bed with my Saul Bellow, while the world believed I was out cruising with Mick Jagger; other times, I couldn't escape the suspicion that I was only cheating myself with my duplicitous behavior. Often, on leaving the clubs, instead of feeling superior to the knot of people outside petitioning to be let in, I thought I ought to join them and realize my potential for a full, rich nightlife.

I got the chance when I visited a friend in Los Angeles. This woman did not know what a yawn was. She put in a full day in the film business and used the night to improve herself (playing tennis under the klieg lights and going to the beauty salon) and to do her chores (the launderette and the supermarket). Spending time with her, I realized just how limiting my need for sleep was: I could be using the wee small hours to take sewing courses and catch up on the ironing. I determined to join her on her nightly rounds, even if I had to prepare for them by sleeping on the beach all day.

I abandoned my plan the very first night. It was terrible to wake up the next morning with the realization that I had dozed off at a 2 AM lecture on colonic irrigation at the twenty-four-hour health spa, staggered home, and once again put in eight hours sleeping.

Of course, I am battling a belief we have held for eight centuries that a third of one's life should be spent in sleep. The man who first made this recommendation was Maimonides, the medieval rabbi, whose medical advice was eagerly followed by sultans and kings. He may simply have prescribed this regimen to afford a breather to the Jews from the steady oppression these Christian and Muslim potentates were apt to mete out during waking hours. In any event, it still has nearly universal acceptance.

Experts say that the older you get, the less sleep you need, so perhaps what I have missed at one end of my life — I rarely stayed out all night even when I was young — I'll get at the other. It is rather frightening to think of myself continually staying up late, desperately looking for ways to fill the darkest hours. And what of love? Wasn't bedtime made for it?

I used to think so, believing that once I had grown up, I would shed such encumbrances as nighties and frolic away in the nude. This view was confirmed by a song, popular at the time, called "Boa Noitte." In my cockney innocence, I thought it was "Buy a Nightie." In the lyrics, this was the advice given by a man to his sweetheart as he urged her to purchase the garment as a kind of chastity belt in his absence:

> *I'll dream my way into your arms again*
> *So buy a nightie until then.*

None of us will need to make such a purchase if current trends continue and we all cut back on sleeping, since I presume that the nightie and all other accoutrements of slumber — mattresses, sheets, pillowcases, alarm clocks, lullabies, quilts, bedtime stories, and on and on — will become obsolete.

When I think of it that way — when I consider that we'll have to fit our dreams and nightmares into our sleepless schedules — I have only one thing to say.

Wake me when it's over.

Watch This Space

"Would you like to be in my movie?" Les Blank, the documentary filmmaker asked, and I thought how ironic it was that the very thing that had once kept me behind the cameras might now put me before them.

Les was contemplating a film about people with gap teeth, but he decided to go ahead without me, because I never heard from him again. In any event, I wasn't disappointed. I'd just as soon not be singled out for my teeth.

Ever since I have had them, I have had the gap. In my childhood pictures, my teeth are unself-consciously, even ostentatiously, displayed. In England then, as now, if you had strong teeth and they were white, you already had more than you were entitled to. It wasn't until I reached my teens and had dreams of stardom that I started making sure my mouth snapped shut before the shutter did. At the time, I was performing with an actors' group so rotten that I stood out like a gold tooth and was pulled by a talent scout, who sent me to meet a Hollywood producer.

Chattering away, I thought I was dazzling the mogul until I paused for breath. Instead of saying, "Sign here," he said: "Fix your teeth."

I was bewildered. Fix my teeth? I thought that was what Hollywood was for. It was a low moment when I realized my credentials weren't impressive enough to justify the investment.

Completely dashed, I was only too willing to listen to a Marxist boyfriend who told me not to bother my head with such decadent bourgeois nonsense and instead to bring my teeth along to the workers' rallies, where they'd never be noticed.

The men in my life have never shown any interest in closing the gap. Both of my husbands considered my teeth serviceable, even cute. But then, many a husband will convince his wife that a glaring defect is an irresistible asset if fixing it's going to cost him money.

I could have paid for my own orthodontist, and when I was on a TV talk show in Canada, almost did. But the producer advised against it. "Your teeth are part of your material," he said. "You can't suddenly appear with your gap closed."

Since my function was to open the show with a funny monologue and then stick around for comic relief, you will see how my teeth were perceived. Was is possible that because of them I could never hope to play a weightier role on the network?

To family and friends (and to anyone who would listen, really), I voiced my concern that my teeth were standing in my way, but everyone advised me against closing the gap or even reducing it.

"You wouldn't be the same," they said — which reminded me of Lady Rosse, who, when she toured an Irish estate, peered into a hut at an old crone sitting up to her knees in pig shit and smoking a clay pipe as she huddled over a fire. "Don't change a thing, dear," Lady Rosse said, "it's absolutely you."

Were my teeth absolutely me? Would my individuality be lost if they were altered? And what if it was? How wonderful to be given a clean slate — something to work with once the gap was no longer a factor in my face! And what other improvements might this new start inspire? Surely I would not continue to be a halfhearted dieter and a feeble exerciser once the possibility of total loveliness lay within my grasp.

Given this prospect, why did I hesitate and finally decide against closing the gap? Well, I hated the idea of capping perfectly sound teeth and giving the world the impression they were not. And then again, how would I look? I have fairly large teeth; if the two front ones were capped to join them, wouldn't they seem enormous? On the other hand, I could wear braces to close the gap, but since my teeth don't protrude, wouldn't they be pointing down my throat by the time they were squeezed together? Wouldn't I have receding teeth?

All these questions would have been eagerly answered by any dentist, but I was unwilling to signal even a slight degree of commitment, so I never asked.

Instead, I stayed with my gap and, as I have been doing since childhood, spread it around. Others may go through magazines adding mustaches; I have brought Garbo, Dietrich, and Monroe down to my level. I have deepened the "aw, shucks" flavor of Gary Cooper's grin, I have made Joan Crawford friendlier-looking, and I have coarsened Madonna by widening her slight gap — a feature, incidentally, like

Rosanna Arquette's overbite and Isabella Rossellini's chip, that shows how one person's dental flaws can be another's charming imperfection. (Rob Lowe might try a gap to mar those perfect looks he is said to find such a burden.)

It gives me particular pleasure to pick up my pencil and have a go at those I think might resent it — the William F. Buckleys, Mick Jagger, Paloma Picasso, Ron and Nancy. I am indebted to Queen Elizabeth for the number of opportunities I've had to gap her: there might have been far fewer if she herself didn't ask portraitists, "Do you want me with or without teeth?"

This was not a question monarchs or anyone else asked much before this century, or even pre-Hollywood. Until the movies inspired stunning advances in cosmetic dentistry, most of us kept our teeth behind closed mouths. Going back through history, if we want dental details, we have to rely on written records. We know the Wife of Bath was "gat-toothed" because Chaucer told us so. But what of Chaucer himself — not to mention Shakespeare, Bach, Catherine the Great?

Even until comparatively recently, teeth have been a mystery. Did you know Al Jolson had gap teeth? At least in private life. Perhaps he covered the gap for the camera as Lauren Hutton sometimes does. Lauren *could* be gapless at all times, but the fact that she chooses not to be suggests that, like gap-toothed Eddie Murphy, David Letterman, Robin Williams, and the late British comic actor Terry-Thomas, she's a joker at heart.

Terry's gap was insured against closing by Lloyd's of London. It was just a publicity gimmick, of course; a gap like his will never close of its own accord. There are some gaps that will close naturally, but they do so in childhood.

Mostly, though, closing the gap takes orthodontic intervention, and without it there would be a lot more people in the world with gap teeth. In fact, so widespread is the use of braces or retainers that nowadays, gap teeth on grown-ups are apt to look childish.

One day, gap teeth may be phased out altogether; but until then, their last acceptable refuge appears to be in the mouths of those adults who not only have a strong silly streak but don't care who knows it. For the inescapable fact is that gap teeth are deeply *Howdy Doody*, and the chances of being called on to read the nightly news, get elected president, or play a love scene with Harrison Ford are virtually nonexistent if you have them.

Believe me, I know. There may be many, many reasons why these and other options weren't open to me, but none could have been more important than my refusal to grit my teeth, bite the bullet, and close the gap.

The Real Thing

The man who invented nylon, Dr. Wallace Hume Carothers, killed himself twenty days after the patent was granted.

He didn't even know that the stuff he'd made out of coal, air, and water was *called* nylon. That wasn't decided until eighteen months later, when the Du Pont people, playing around with the word *no-run* (because the first use of the fiber was in stockings), hit on *nylon*.

Julian W. Hill, Dr. Carothers's assistant, is still alive at this writing. At the age of eighty-three, he turned up at the fiftieth-anniversary celebration of nylon in January 1988 and told the *Washington Post:* "I think the human race is going to perish by being smothered in plastic."

The Du Pont people must have been furious. I can't say I was too pleased myself. Particularly since he'd been in there at the birth, I wish Mr. Hill hadn't taken this opportunity to remind us how nylon turned out.

I still think of the days when, to me, the hope of the world was with America, where everyone was equal and modern, and where nylon, which never bagged or sagged, was glamorous, sexy, sheer, and everlasting — unlike England, which was riddled with class distinctions and old-fashioned natural fibers that shrank and stretched, felted and matted, withered and rotted away.

I never felt closer to skyscrapers, sundaes, and stardom than when I put on my first pair of nylons. At last, I could imagine myself sailing away to the land of legs and posing for eager photographers upon my arrival, skirt raised like a starlet, as if showing my entry visa.

Since then, I have often wished there weren't a price to pay for putting Nature in her place. How I have wished that the crackle of static had never been sounded, that I had never laid eyes on the ugly American in polyester, and, most of all, that nylon had not turned out to be everlasting.

Every setback I have noticed in the steady advance of synthetics has seemed like a victory for those class-conscious English environmentalists in their pure tweeds who used to call me a "dreadful little cockney" when they found my ice-cream wrappers on the beach. People like that, on both sides of the Atlantic, probably think poor old Carothers killed himself not because he was a manic-depressive, but because he realized he hadn't delivered the future, he had brought forth the apocalypse.

If only he had lived to show up at the fiftieth-anniversary party and, at the age of ninety-one, announce: "Thank God Styrofoam boxes *aren't* biodegradable, because I've found a way to make them edible and now they can be eaten right along with the Big Mac or shipped overseas to feed starving millions. As for toxic waste, it isn't poisonous after all and can, in fact, cure anything you care to think of — and, of course, these fallout medical benefits won't cost a penny."

If Dr. Carothers were alive, he wouldn't have made these

discoveries alone, as he and Mr. Hill did with nylon, but in a group working on a project with an awful name like Genesis 2000, an enterprise that has got today's geneticists and biochemists busy trying to find out how we're made so that parts of us can be duplicated. They've already come up with Dacron veins; soon we may get never-fail nylon livers, and kidneys that can be slipped into our systems as easily as false teeth are slid into our mouths.

"I love *everything* artificial," I said as a teenager to emphasize to Colin, an outdoorsy British lad, that he didn't stand a chance with me and my nylons.

"Well, you'll get it with them bloody Yanks," he said.

I still hope so.

Junk Blond

I didn't become a blond until I grew up and became gray. If I'd gone blond sooner, I would have had dark roots, and in those prepunk days, telltale roots weren't stylish.

During my teenage years, I dreamed of transforming myself from commonplace brunette to glamorous blond as soon as I left school. What stopped me was the fear that as a blond bombshell I could misfire: instead of being regarded as clever and classy, I could be dismissed as dumb and cheap.

Mental aptitude isn't tied to hair color as it once was, but I still earn the label "cheap blond," since I buy whatever dye costs the least and slap it on in a way no expensive colorist ever would. Mostly, what I am doing is bleaching my hair, although with my slapdash approach I never quite manage total coverage. I am a blond who has more fun — at least as far as turning blond is concerned. I spray, shampoo, and paint, taking childish delight in getting almost instant results with minimal effort and skill.

Because it's less of a contrast to my natural gray, going blond has seemed almost like natural evolution, particularly now that I have no current Hollywood substitute for my teenage dream of Veronica Lake. Just the same, I'm by no means committed to blond. Last winter, I was, briefly, a redhead. But the effect was less incendiary than I'd hoped, so I went back to blond. Now my gray hairs — there are always quite a few uncovered — are giving me ideas.

Perhaps gray is the wave of the future ("Crave that gray? Spray on Today!"), just as it was two centuries ago, when Marie Antoinette dusted her blond hair with gray powder. I notice Elizabeth Taylor is using gray for highlights; and when *Life* shot a gown from Lacroix, the new king of couture, the model had a gray pompadour. Clairol says blonds like me will want to be warmer (less white, more yellow) this winter, so maybe I will wrap a few strands of gray in foil, color the rest, and go for silver threads among the gold.

Most colorists say you ought to go lighter as you get older because it has a softening effect. There are women in the world who don't give a damn about that. Gloria Vanderbilt and Mary McFadden grow more obdurately brunette with the passing years in the interest of maintaining their formidable fashion images, which even a hint of light at the temples could dim.

I am glad that I am not known by my hair and can color it cinnamon whenever I feel like it. And I am glad that although the world has gotten worse in most ways, in the matter of hair coloring there has been nothing but improvement. Today, it's so easy that anyone can manage it. I know that I never feel the slightest trepidation in trying something new. If the chartreuse fails to deliver the shimmer but makes my skin look green instead, I can shampoo it out as easily as taking off my makeup.

It was probably just as easy when I first started dyeing

261

my hair in the mid-1960s, but I had grown cautious since my blond-crazed youth and I dreaded taking the first step. Timidly, I went to a neighborhood parlor where, I felt, they were not likely to be extremist. I was further reassured when I was shown an enormous selection of browns, each one but a nuance apart from the other. Why go to fancy joints, I asked myself, when service like this was available above the hardware store? The answer soon came. The selection of shade was a mere formality. My hair emerged black as the treacherous heart of my second husband, whose womanizing ways had driven me to dye in the first place.

"We make it dense at first," the colorist said, "so it will stand up to shampoos."

It stood up all right. In fact, it was downright indelible. Fortunately, I became attached to it. Colorists claim hair tints can act cosmetically — minimize double chains, lift low foreheads, reduce prominent noses, and so on. I found out that my raven locks, combined with pale makeup and loads of mascara and eyeliner, gave me a look at once soulful and bewitching — just what was needed for a reproachful confrontation with my spouse.

It took him a while to notice. When he did, instead of saying, "Darling, I never appreciated your porcelain loveliness before now — how could I have thought anyone more appealing?" he remarked: "You're looking peaked. You ought to get outdoors more."

After that first mishap, I used dyes that returned me to my own color while I remained with my husband. But once we divorced, I discovered the truth of the ad that says dyeing your hair "let's me be me" — especially when it's not your own color. In fact, I wish my passport said "dyed blond" instead of "blond," because it's certainly a label I bear proudly and one that fits me from head to toe. Indeed, I have never restricted hair dyeing only to my head. I just wish minikits were available, so I could really experiment with my eyebrows instead of using the dregs left over from the regular package.

Although my hair is mostly in my own hands, one of these days I'm going to treat myself to a dimensional dye job by an expert and perhaps get a tea-colored tint with peach and platinum streaks. Maybe I'll even go to a salon where they stencil-stripe or dot or tease your hair down to the base and just color the tips.

Clairol says its scientists will one day be experimenting with laser beams as a substitute for the sun and manipulating melanin, the pigment that colors skin and hair, with the aim of effecting gradual, discreet change.

I'm sure many will be pleased, but I don't believe the better part of color is discretion. Brazen's best, I think: thrilling to the sight of a spiky punk do colored pink and silver. Now, that's liberating your locks, and *that* (pass the sparkling magenta spray, please) is for me.

Acknowledgments

My grateful thanks to my editor, Pat Mulcahy, and my agent, Liz Darhansoff.

Mary Peacock, Abby Thomas, Iona Monahan, Avril Showell, and Bronwen Meredith may never know how much I owe them. Although they probably have a good idea.